CHESTER RAND

or, The New Path to Fortune

I0667599

HORATIO ALGER, Jr.

1st WORLD
LIBRARY
Literary Society

Chester Rand

Horatio Alger, Jr

© 1st World Library, 2009
PO Box 2211
Fairfield, IA 52556
www.1stworldlibrary.com
First Edition

LCCN: 2009923399

Softcover ISBN: 978-1-4218-8848-4
Hardcover ISBN: 978-1-4218-8947-4
eBook ISBN: 978-1-4218-8749-4

Purchase *"Chester Rand"*
as a traditional bound book at:
www.1stWorldLibrary.com/purchase.asp?ISBN=978-1-4218-8848-4

1st World Library is a literary, educational organization
dedicated to:

- Creating a free internet library of downloadable ebooks

- Hosting writing competitions and offering book publishing
scholarships.

Interested in more 1st World Library books? contact:
literacy@1stworldlibrary.com
Check us out at: www.1stworldlibrary.com

1ˢᵗ World Library Literary Society

Giving Back to the World

"If you want to work on the core problem, it's early school literacy."

- James Barksdale, former CEO of Netscape

"No skill is more crucial to the future of a child, or to a democratic and prosperous society, than literacy."

- Los Angeles Times

"Literacy... means far more than learning how to read and write... The aim is to transmit... knowledge and promote social participation."

- UNESCO

"Literacy is not a luxury, it is a right and a responsibility. If our world is to meet the challenges of the twenty-first century we must harness the energy and creativity of all our citizens."

- President Bill Clinton

"Parents should be encouraged to read to their children, and teachers should be equipped with all available techniques for teaching literacy, so the varying needs and capacities of individual kids can be taken into account."

- Hugh Mackay

CONTENTS

CHAPTER I

SILAS TRIPP

Probably the best known citizen of Wyncombe, a small town nestling among the Pennsylvania mountains, was Silas Tripp. He kept the village store, occasionally entertained travelers, having three spare rooms, was town treasurer, and conspicuous in other local offices.

The store was in the center of the village, nearly opposite the principal church—there were two—and here it was that the townspeople gathered to hear and discuss the news.

Silas Tripp had one assistant, a stout, pleasant-looking boy of fifteen, who looked attractive, despite his well-worn suit. Chester Rand was the son of a widow, who lived in a tiny cottage about fifty rods west of the Presbyterian church, of which, by the way, Silas Tripp was senior deacon, for he was a leader in religious as well as secular affairs.

Chester's father had died of pneumonia about four years before the story commences, leaving his widow the cottage and about two hundred and fifty dollars. This sum little by little had melted, and a month previous the last dollar had been spent for the winter's supply of coal.

Mrs. Rand had earned a small income by plain sewing and binding shoes for a shoe shop in the village, but to her dismay the announcement had just been made that the shop would close through the winter on account of the increased price of leather and overproduction during the year.

"What shall we do, Chester?" she asked, in alarm, when the news came. "We can't live on your salary, and I get very little sewing to do."

"No, mother," said Chester, his own face reflecting her anxiety; "we can't live on three dollars a week."

"I have been earning two dollars by binding shoes," said Mrs. Rand. "It has been hard enough to live on five dollars a week, but I don't know how we can manage on three."

"I'll tell you what I'll do, mother. I'll ask Mr. Tripp to raise my pay to four dollars a week."

"But will he do it? He is a very close man, and always pleading poverty."

"But I happen to know that he has ten thousand dollars invested in Pennsylvania Railroad stock. I overheard him saying so to Mr. Gardner."

"Ten thousand dollars! It seems a fortune!" sighed Mrs. Rand. "Why do some people have so much and others so little?"

"It beats me, mother. But I don't think either of us would exchange places with Silas Tripp with all his money. By the way, mother, Mr. Tripp is a widower. Why don't you set your cap for him?"

Mrs. Rand smiled, as her imagination conjured up the weazened and wrinkled face of the village storekeeper, with his gray hair standing up straight on his head like a natural pompadour.

"If you want Mr. Tripp for a stepfather," she said, "I will see what I can do to ingratiate myself with him."

"No, a thousand times no!" replied Chester, with a shudder. "I'd rather live on one meal a day than have you marry him."

"I agree with you, Chester. We will live for each other, and hope for something to turn up."

"I hope the first thing to turn up will be an increase of salary. To-morrow is New Year's Day, and it will be a good time to ask."

Accordingly, that evening, just as the store was about to close, Chester gathered up courage and said: "Mr. Tripp."

"Well, that's my name," said Silas, looking over his iron-bowed spectacles.

"To-morrow is New Year's Day."

"What if 'tis? I reckon I knew that without your tellin' me."

"I came here last New Year's Day. I've been here a year."

"What if you have?"

"And I thought perhaps you might be willing to raise my salary to four dollars a week," continued Chester, hurriedly.

"Oho, that's what you're after, is it?" said Silas, grimly. "You think I'm made of money, I reckon. Now, don't you?"

"No, I don't; but, Mr. Tripp, mother and I find it very hard to get along, really we do. She won't have any more shoes to bind for three months to come, on account of the shoe shop's closing."

"It's going to hurt me, too," said Silas, with a frown. "When one business suspends it affects all the rest. I'll have mighty hard work to make both ends meet."

This struck Chester as ludicrous, but he did not feel inclined to laugh. Here was Silas Tripp gathering in trade from the entire village and getting not a little in addition from outlying towns, complaining that he would find it hard to make both ends meet, though everyone said that he did not spend one-third of his income. On the whole, things did not look very encouraging.

"Perhaps," he said, nervously, "you would raise me to three dollars and a half?"

"What is the boy thinkin' of? You must think I'm made of money. Why, three dollars is han'some pay for what little you do."

"Why, I work fourteen hours a day," retorted Chester.

"I'm afraid you're gettin' lazy. Boys shouldn't complain of their work. The fact is, Chester, I feel as if I was payin' you too much."

"Too much! Three dollars a week too much!"

"Too much, considerin' the state of business, and yourself bein' a boy. I've been meanin' to tell you that I've got a chance to get a cheaper boy."

"Who is it?" asked Chester, in dismay.

"It's Abel Wood. Abel Wood is every mite as big and strong as you are, and he come round last evenin' and said he'd work for two dollars and a quarter a week."

"I couldn't work for that," said Chester.

"I don't mind bein' generous, considerin' you've been working for me more than a year. I'll give you two dollars and a half. That's twenty-five cents more'n the Wood boy is willin' to take."

"Abel Wood doesn't know anything about store work."

"I'll soon learn him. Sitooated as I am, I feel that I must look after every penny," and Mr. Tripp's face looked meaner and more weazened than ever as he fixed his small, bead-like eyes on his boy clerk.

"Then I guess I'll have to leave you, Mr. Tripp," said Chester, with a deep feeling of disgust and dismay.

"Do just as you like," said his employer. "You're on reasonnable to expect to get high pay when business is dull."

"High pay!" repeated Chester, bitterly. "Three dollars a week!"

"It's what I call high pay. When I was a boy, I only earned two dollars a week."

"Money would go further when you were a boy."

"Yes, it did. Boys wasn't so extravagant in them days."

"I don't believe you were ever extravagant, Mr. Tripp," said Chester, with a tinge of sarcasm which his employer didn't detect.

"No, I wasn't. I don't want to brag, but I never spent a cent foolishly. Do you know how much money I spent the first three months I was at work?"

"A dollar?" guessed Chester.

"A dollar!" repeated Mr. Tripp, in a tone of disapproval. "No, I only spent thirty-seven cents."

"Then I don't wonder you got rich," said Chester, with a curl of the lip.

"I ain't rich," said Silas Tripp, cautiously. "Who told you I was?"

"Everybody says so."

"Then everybody is wrong. I'm a leetle 'forehanded, that's all."

"I've heard people say you could afford to give up work and live on the interest of your money."

Silas Tripp held up his hands as if astounded.

"'Tain't so," he said, sharply. "If I gave up business, I'd soon be in the poorhouse. Well, what do you say? Will you stay along and work for two dollars and a half a week?"

"I couldn't do it," said Chester, troubled.

"All right! It's jest as you say. Your week ends to-morrow night. If you see Abel Wood, you can tell him I want to see him."

"I will," answered Chester, bitterly.

As he walked home he felt very despondent. Wouldn't it have been better, he asked himself, to accept reduced wages than to give up his job? It would have been hard enough to attempt living on two dollars and a half a week, but that was better than no income at all. And yet, it looked so mean in Silas Tripp to present such an alternative, when he was abundantly able to give him the increase he asked for.

"I must tell mother and see what she thinks about it," he said to himself.

CHAPTER II

OUT OF WORK

Chester had a talk with his mother that evening. She felt indignant at Silas Tripp's meanness, but advised Chester to remain in the store for the present.

"I'd rather work anywhere else for two dollars," said Chester, bitterly.

It would be humiliating enough to accept the reduction, but he felt that duty to his mother required the sacrifice. He started on his way to the store in the morning, prepared to notify Mr. Tripp that he would remain, but he found that it was too late. Just before he reached the store, he met Abel Wood, a loose-jointed, towheaded boy, with a stout body and extraordinarily long legs, who greeted him with a grin.

"I'm goin' to work in your place Monday mornin'," he said.

"Has Mr. Tripp spoken to you?" asked Chester, his heart sinking.

"Yes, he said you was goin' to leave. What's up?"

"Mr. Tripp cut down my wages," said Chester. "I couldn't

work for two dollars and a half."

"He's only goin' to give me two and a quarter."

"You can afford to work for that. Your father's got steady work."

"Yes, but all the same I'll ask for more in a few weeks. Where are you goin' to work?"

"I don't know yet," answered Chester, sadly.

"It's awful hard to get a place in Wyncombe."

"I suppose it is. I hope something will turn up."

He tried to speak hopefully, but there was very little hope in his heart.

He went about his work in a mechanical way, but neglected nothing. When the time came for the store to close, Silas Tripp took three dollars from the drawer and handed it to him, saying: "There's your wages, Chester. I expect it's the last I'll pay you."

"Yes, sir, I suppose so."

"I don't know how I'll like the Wood boy. He hain't no experience."

"He'll get it, sir."

"If you want to stay for two and a quarter—the same I'm going to give him—I'll tell him I've changed my mind."

"No, sir; it wouldn't be right to put him off now. I guess I'll get something else to do."

He turned and left the store, walking with a slower step than usual. His heart was heavy, for he felt that, poorly as they lived hitherto, they must live more poorly still in the days to come. He reached home at last, and put the three dollars in his mother's hands.

"I don't know when I shall have any more money to give you, mother," he said.

"It looks dark, Chester, but the Lord reigns. He will still be our friend."

There was something in these simple words that cheered Chester, and a weight seemed lifted from his heart. He felt that they were not quite friendless, and that there was still One, kinder and more powerful than any earthly friend, to whom they could look for help.

When Monday morning came he rose at the usual hour and breakfasted.

"I'll go out and take a walk, mother," he said. "Perhaps I may find some work somewhere."

Almost unconsciously, he took the familiar way to the store, and paused at a little distance from it. He saw Abel come out with some packages to carry to a customer. It pained him to see another boy in his place, and he turned away with a sigh.

During the night four or five inches of snow had fallen. This gave him an idea. As he came to the house of the Misses Cleveland, two maiden sisters who lived in a small cottage set back fifty feet from the road, he opened the gate and went up to the front door.

Horatio Alger, Jr

Miss Jane Cleveland opened it for him.

"Good-morning, Chester," she said.

"Good-morning, Miss Cleveland. I thought you might want to get a path shoveled to the gate."

"So I would; Hannah tried to do it last time it snowed, but she caught an awful cold. But ain't you working up at the store?"

"Not now. Mr. Tripp cut down my wages, and I left."

"Do tell. Have you got another place?"

"Not just yet. I thought I'd do any little jobs that came along till I got one."

"That's right. What'll you charge to shovel a path?"

Chester hesitated.

"Fifteen cents," he answered, at last.

"I'll give you ten. Money's skerce."

Chester reflected that he could probably do the job in half an hour, and he accepted. It cheered him to think he was earning something, however small.

He worked with a will, and in twenty-five minutes the work was done.

"You're spry," said Jane Cleveland, when he brought the shovel to the door. "It took Hannah twice as long, and she didn't do it as well."

"It isn't the kind of work for ladies," replied Chester.

"Wait till I fetch the money."

Miss Cleveland went into the house, and returned with a nickel and four pennies.

"I'm reely ashamed," she said. "I'll have to owe you a cent. But here's a mince pie I've just baked. Take it home to your ma. Maybe it'll come handy. I'll try to think of the other cent next time you come along."

"Don't trouble yourself about it, Miss Cleveland. The pie is worth a good deal more than the cent. Mother'll be very much obliged to you."

"She's very welcome, I'm sure," said the kindly spinster. "I hope you'll get work soon, Chester."

"Thank you."

Chester made his way homeward, as he did not care to carry the pie about with him. His mother looked at him in surprise as he entered the house.

"What have you there, Chester?" she asked.

"A pie from Miss Cleveland."

"But how came she to give you a pie?"

"I shoveled a path for her, and she gave me a pie and ten cents—no, nine. So you see, mother, I've earned something this week."

"I take it as a good omen. A willing hand will generally find

Horatio Alger, Jr

work to do."

"How are you off for wood, mother?"

"There is some left, Chester."

"I'll go out in the yard and work at the wood pile till dinner time. Then this afternoon I will go out again and see if I can find some more paths to shovel."

But Chester was not destined to earn any more money that day. As a general thing, the village people shoveled their own paths, and would regard hiring such work done as sinful extravagance. Chester did, however, find some work to do. About half-past three he met Abel Wood tugging a large basket, filled with groceries, to the minister's house. He had set it down, and was resting his tired arms when Chester came along.

"Give me a lift with this basket, Chester, that's a good fellow," said Abel.

Chester lifted it.

"Yes, it is heavy," he said.

"The minister's got some company," went on Abel, "and he's given an extra large order."

"How do you like working in the store, Abel?"

"It's hard work, harder than I thought."

"But remember what a magnificent salary you will get," said Chester, with a smile.

"It ain't half enough. Say, Chester, old Tripp is rich, ain't he?"

"I should call myself rich if I had his money."

"He's a miserly old hunks, then, to give me such small pay."

"Don't let him hear you say so."

"I'll take care of that. Come, you'll help me, won't you?"

"Yes," answered Chester, good-naturedly; "I might as well, as I have nothing else to do."

Between the two the basket was easily carried. In a short time they had reached the minister's house. They took the basket around to the side door, just as Mr. Morris, the minister, came out, accompanied by a young man, who was evidently a stranger in the village, as Chester did not remember having seen him before.

"Chester," said the minister, kindly, "how does it happen that you have an assistant to-day?"

"I am the assistant, Mr. Morris. Abel is Mr. Tripp's new boy."

"Indeed, I am surprised to hear that. When did you leave the store?"

"Last Saturday night."

"Have you another place?"

"Not yet."

"Are you at leisure this afternoon?"

"Yes, sir."

"Then perhaps you will walk around with my friend, Mr. Conrad, and show him the village. I was going with him, but I have some writing to do, and you will do just as well."

"I shall be very happy to go with Mr. Conrad," said Chester, politely.

"And I shall be very glad to have you," said the young man, with a pleasant smile.

"Come back to supper, Chester," said the minister; "that is, if your mother can spare you."

"Thank you, sir. I suppose you will be able to carry back the empty basket, Abel," added Chester, as his successor emerged from the side door, relieved of his burden.

"I guess so," answered Abel, with a grin.

"I was never in Wyncombe before," began Mr. Conrad, "though I am a second cousin of your minister, Mr. Morris. I have to go away to-morrow morning, and wish to see a little of the town while I am here."

"Where do you live, Mr. Conrad?"

"In the city of New York."

"Are you a minister, too?"

"Oh, no!" laughed the young man. "I am in a very different business. I am an artist—in a small way. I make sketches for books and magazines."

"And does that pay?"

"Fairly well. I earn a comfortable living."

"I didn't know one could get money for making pictures. I like to draw, myself."

"I will see what you can do this evening; that is, if you accept my cousin's invitation."

Before the walk was over Chester had become much interested in his new friend. He listened eagerly to his stories of the great city, and felt that life must be much better worth living there than in Wyncombe.

CHAPTER III

A NOTEWORTHY EVENING

Chester enjoyed his supper. Mr. Morris, though a minister, had none of the starched dignity that many of his profession think it necessary to assume. He was kindly and genial, with a pleasant humor that made him agreeable company for the young as well as the old. Mr. Conrad spoke much of New York and his experiences there, and Chester listened to him eagerly.

"You have never been to New York, Chester?" said the young artist.

"No, sir, but I have read about it—and dreamed about it. Sometime I hope to go there."

"I think that is the dream of every country boy. Well, it is the country boys that make the most successful men."

"How do you account for that, Herbert?" asked the minister.

"Generally they have been brought up to work, and work more earnestly than the city boys."

When the supper table was cleared, Mr. Conrad took from

his valise two or three of the latest issues of *Puck*, *Judge* and *Life*. He handed them to Chester, who looked over them eagerly.

"Do you ever contribute to these papers, Mr. Conrad?" he asked.

"Yes; here is a sketch in *Judge*, and another in *Life*, which I furnished."

"And do you get good pay for them?"

"I received ten dollars for each."

Chester's eyes opened with surprise.

"Why," he said, "they are small. It couldn't have taken you long to draw them."

"Probably half an hour for each one."

"And you received ten dollars each?"

"Yes, but don't gauge such work by the time it takes. It is the idea that is of value. The execution is a minor matter."

Chester looked thoughtful.

"I should like to be an artist," he said, after a pause.

"Won't you give me a specimen of your work? You have seen mine."

"I have not done any comic work, but I think I could."

"Here is a piece of drawing paper. Now, let me see what you

Horatio Alger, Jr

can do."

Chester leaned his head on his hand and began to think. He was in search of an idea. The young artist watched him with interest. At last his face brightened up. He seized the pencil, and began to draw rapidly. In twenty minutes he handed the paper to Mr. Conrad.

The latter looked at it in amazement.

"Why, you are an artist," he said. "I had no idea you were capable of such work."

"I am glad you like it," said Chester, much pleased.

"How long have you been drawing?"

"Ever since I can remember. I used to make pictures in school on my slate. Some of them got me into trouble with the teacher."

"I can imagine it, if you caricatured him. Did you ever take lessons?"

"No; there was no one in Wyncombe to teach me. But I got hold of a drawing book once, and that helped me."

"Do you know what I am going to do with this sketch of yours?"

Chester looked an inquiry.

"I will take it to New York with me, and see if I can dispose of it."

"I am afraid it won't be of much use, Mr. Conrad. I am only

a boy."

"If a sketch is good, it doesn't matter how old or young an artist is."

"I should like very much to get something for it. Even fifty cents would be acceptable."

"You hold your talent cheap, Chester," said Mr. Conrad, with a smile. "I shall certainly ask more than that for it, as I don't approve of cheapening artistic labor."

The rest of the evening passed pleasantly.

When Chester rose to go, Mr. Conrad said:

"Take these papers, Chester. You can study them at your leisure, and if any happy thoughts or brilliant ideas come to you, dash them off and send them to me. I might do something with them."

"Thank you, sir. What is your address?"

"Number one ninety-nine West Thirty-fourth Street. Well, good-by. I am glad to have met you. Sometime you may be an artist."

Chester flushed with pride, and a new hope rose in his breast. He had always enjoyed drawing, but no one had ever encouraged him in it. Even his mother thought of it only as a pleasant diversion for him. As to its bringing him in money, the idea had never occurred to him.

It seemed wonderful, indeed, that a little sketch, the work of half an hour, should bring ten dollars. Why compare with this the hours of toil in a grocery store—seventy, at least—

which had been necessary to earn the small sum of three dollars. For the first time Chester began to understand the difference between manual and intelligent labor.

It was ten o'clock when Chester left the minister's house—a late hour in Wyncombe—and he had nearly reached his own modest home before he met anyone. Then he overtook a man of perhaps thirty, thinly clad and shivering in the bitter, wintry wind. He was a stranger, evidently, for Chester knew everyone in the village, and he was tempted to look back. The young man, encouraged perhaps by this evidence of interest, spoke, hurriedly:

"Do you know," he asked, "where I can get a bed for the night?"

"Mr. Tripp has a few rooms that he lets to strangers. He is the storekeeper."

The young man laughed, but there was no merriment in the laugh.

"Oh, yes. I know Silas Tripp," he said.

"Then you have been in Wyncombe before?"

"I never lived here, but I know Silas Tripp better than I want to. He is my uncle."

"Your uncle!" exclaimed Chester, in surprise.

"Yes, I am his sister's son. My name is Walter Bruce."

"Then I should think your uncle's house was the place for you."

"I have no money to pay for a bed."

"But, if you are a relation—"

"That makes no difference to Silas Tripp. He has no love for poor relations. You don't know him very well."

"I ought to, for I have worked for him in the store for a year."

"I didn't see you in there this evening."

"I left him last Saturday evening. There is another boy there now."

"Why did you leave him?"

"Because he wanted to cut down my wages from three dollars to two dollars and a quarter."

"Just like uncle Silas. I see you know him."

"Have you seen him since you came to Wyncombe?"

"I was in the store this evening."

"Did you make yourself known to him?"

"Yes."

"Didn't he invite you to spend the night in the house?"

"Not he. He saw by my dress that I was poor, and gave me a lecture on my shiftless ways."

"Still he might have taken care of you for one night."

"He wouldn't. He told me he washed his hands of me."

Chester looked sober. He was shocked by Silas Tripp's want of humanity.

"You asked me where you could find a bed," he said. "Come home with me, and I can promise you shelter for one night, at least."

"Thank you, boy," said Bruce, grasping Chester's hand. "You have a heart. But—perhaps your parents might object."

"I have no father. My mother is always ready to do a kind act."

"Then I will accept your kind offer. I feared I should have to stay out all night."

"And without an overcoat," said Chester, compassionately.

"Yes, I had to part with my overcoat long since. I could not afford such a luxury. I suppose you understand!"

"You sold it?"

"No, I pawned it. I didn't get much for it—only three dollars, but it would be as easy for me to take the church and move it across the street as to redeem it."

"You appear to have been unfortunate."

"Yes. Fortune and I are at odds. Yet I ought to have some money."

"How's that?"

"When my mother died uncle Silas acted as executor of her estate. It was always supposed that she had some money— probably from two to three thousand dollars—but when uncle Silas rendered in his account it had dwindled to one hundred and twenty-five dollars. Of course that didn't last me long."

"Do you think that he acted wrongfully?" asked Chester, startled.

"Do I think so? I have no doubt of it. You know money is his god."

"Yet to cheat his own nephew would be so base."

"Is there anything too base for such a man to do to get money?"

The young man spoke bitterly.

By this time they had reached Chester's home. His mother was still up. She looked up in surprise at her son's companion.

"Mother," said Chester, "this is Mr. Bruce. Do you think we can give him a bed?"

"Why, certainly," replied Mrs. Rand, cordially. "Have you had supper, sir?"

"I wouldn't like to trouble you, ma'am."

"It will be no trouble. I can make some tea in five minutes. Chester, take out the bread and butter and cold meat from the closet."

So before he went to bed the homeless wayfarer was

provided with a warm meal, and the world seemed brighter and more cheerful to him.

CHAPTER IV

A DYING GIFT

In the morning Walter Bruce came down to breakfast looking pale and sick. He had taken a severe cold from scanty clothing and exposure to the winter weather.

"You have a hard cough, Mr. Bruce," said Mrs. Rand, in a tone of sympathy.

"Yes, madam; my lungs were always sensitive."

When breakfast was over he took his hat and prepared to go.

"I thank you very much for your kind hospitality," he began. Then he was attacked by a fit of coughing.

"Where are you going. Mr. Bruce?" asked Chester.

"I don't know," he answered, despondently. "I came to Wyncombe to see my uncle Silas, but he will have nothing to say to me."

Chester and his mother exchanged looks. The same thought was in the mind of each.

"Stay with us a day or two," said Mrs. Rand. "You are not fit to travel. You need rest and care."

"But I shall be giving you a great deal of trouble."

"We shall not consider it such," said Mrs. Rand.

"Then I will accept your kind offer, for indeed I am very unwell."

Before the end of the day the young man was obliged to go to bed, and a doctor was summoned. Bruce was pronounced to have a low fever, and to be quite unfit to travel.

Mrs. Rand and Chester began to feel anxious. Their hearts were filled with pity for the young man, but how could they bear the expense which this sickness would entail upon them?

"Silas Tripp is his uncle," said Mrs. Rand. "He ought to contribute the expense of his sickness."

"I will go and see him," said Chester. So he selected a time when business would be slack in the store, and called in. He found Mr. Trip in a peevish mood.

"How are you, Chester?" he said. "I wish you was back."

"Why, Mr. Tripp? You've got Abel Wood in my place."

"He ain't of much account," grumbled Silas. "What do you think he done this mornin'?"

"I don't know, sir."

"He smashed two dozen eggs, and eggs twenty-two cents a

dozen. But I'll take it out of his salary. He's dreadful awkward, that boy!"

"Poor Abel!" thought Chester. "I am afraid he won't have much salary coming to him at the end of the week."

"You never broke no eggs while you was here, Chester."

"No; I don't think I did."

"You'd ought to have stayed."

"I couldn't stay on the salary you offered. But, Mr. Tripp, I've come here on business."

"Hey? What about?"

"Your nephew, Walter Bruce, is staying at our house."

"Is he?" returned Silas Tripp, indifferently.

"And he is sick."

"I don't feel no interest in him," said Silas, doggedly.

"Are you willing to pay his expenses? He has no money."

"No, I ain't," snarled Silas. "Ef you take him you take him at your own risk."

"You wouldn't have us turn him into the street?" said Chester, indignantly.

"You can do as you like. It ain't no affair of mine. I s'pose he sent you here."

"No, he didn't; and I wouldn't have come if we had been better fixed. But we haven't enough money to live on ourselves."

"Then tell him to go away. I never wanted him to come to Wyncombe."

"It seems to me you ought to do something for your own nephew."

"I can't support all my relations, and I won't," said Silas, testily. "It ain't no use talkin'. Walter Bruce is shif'less and lazy, or he'd take care of himself. I ain't no call to keep him."

"Then you won't do anything for him? Even two dollars a week would help him very much."

"Two dollars a week!" ejaculated Silas. "You must think I am made of money. Why, two dollars a week would make a hundred and four dollars a year."

"That wouldn't be much for a man of your means, Mr. Tripp."

"You talk foolish, Chester. I have to work hard for a livin'. If I helped all my shif'less relations I'd end my days in the poorhouse."

"I don't think you'll go there from that cause," Chester could not help saying.

"I guess not. I ain't a fool. Let every tub stand on its own bottom, I say. But I won't be too hard. Here's twenty-five cents," and Silas took a battered quarter from the money drawer.

"Take it and use it careful."

"I think we will try to get along without it," said Chester, with a curl of the lip. "I'm afraid you can't afford it."

"Do just as you like," said Silas, putting back the money with a sigh of relief, "but don't say I didn't offer to do something for Walter."

"No; I will tell him how much you offered to give."

"That's a queer boy," said Mr. Tripp, as Chester left the store. "Seems to want me to pay all Walter Bruce's expenses. What made him come to Wyncombe to get sick? He'd better have stayed where he lived, and then he'd have had a claim to go to the poorhouse. He can't live on me, I tell him that. Them Rands are foolish to take him in. They're as poor as poverty themselves, and now they've taken in a man who ain't no claim on them. I expect they thought they'd get a good sum out of me for boardin' him. There's a great many onrasonable people in the world."

"I will go and see Mr. Morris, the minister," decided the perplexed Chester. "He will tell me what to do."

Accordingly he called on the minister and unfolded the story to sympathetic ears.

"You did right, Chester," said Mr. Morris. "The poor fellow was fortunate to fall into your hands. But won't it be too much for your mother?"

"It's the expense I am thinking of, Mr. Morris. You know I have lost my situation, and mother has no shoes to bind."

"I can help you, Chester. A rich lady of my acquaintance

sends me a hundred dollars every year to bestow in charity. I will devote a part of this to the young man whom you have so kindly taken in, say at the rate of eight dollars a week."

"That will make us feel easy," said Chester gratefully. "How much do you think his uncle offered me?"

"I am surprised that he should have offered anything."

"He handed me twenty-five cents, but I told him I thought we could get along without it."

"And you will. Silas Tripp has a small soul, hardly worth saving. He has made money his god, and serves his chosen deity faithfully."

"I wouldn't change places with him for all his wealth."

"Some day you may be as rich as he, but I hope, if you are, you will use your wealth better."

At the beginning of the third week Walter Bruce became suddenly worse. His constitution was fragile, and the disease had undermined his strength. The doctor looked grave.

"Do you think I shall pull through, doctor?" asked the young man.

"While there is life there is hope, Mr. Bruce."

"That means that the odds are against me?"

"Yes, I am sorry to say that you are right."

Walter Bruce looked thoughtful.

"I don't think I care much for life," he said. "I have had many disappointments, and I know that at the best I could never be strong and enjoy life as most of my age do—I am resigned."

"How old are you, Walter?" asked Chester.

"Twenty-nine. It is a short life."

"Is there anyone you would wish me to notify if the worst comes?"

"No, I have scarcely a relative—except Silas Tripp," he added, with a bitter smile.

"You have no property to dispose of by will?" asked the doctor.

"Yes," was the unexpected answer, "but I shall not make a will. A will may be contested. I will give it away during my life."

Chester and the doctor looked surprised. They thought the other might refer to a ring or some small article.

"I want everything to be legal," resumed Bruce. "Is there a lawyer in the village?"

"Yes, Lawyer Gardener."

"Send for him. I shall feel easier when I have attended to this last duty."

Within half an hour the lawyer was at his bedside.

"In the inside pocket of my coat," said Walter Bruce, "you will find a document. It is the deed of five lots in the town of

Tacoma, in Washington Territory. I was out there last year, and having a little money, bought the lots for a song. They are worth very little now, but some time they may be of value."

"To whom do you wish to give them?" asked Mr. Gardner.

"To this boy," answered Bruce, looking affectionately toward Chester. "He and his have been my best friends."

"But your uncle—he is a relative!" suggested Chester.

"He has no claim upon me. Lawyer, make out a deed of gift of these lots to Chester Rand, and I will sign it."

The writing was completed, Bruce found strength to sign it, and then sank back exhausted. Two days later he died. Of course the eight dollars a week from the minister's fund ceased to be paid to the Rands. Chester had not succeeded in obtaining work. To be sure he had the five lots in Tacoma, but he who had formerly owned them had died a pauper. The outlook was very dark.

CHAPTER V

CHESTER'S FIRST SUCCESS

Chester and his mother and a few friends attended the funeral of Walter Bruce. Silas Tripp was too busy at the store to pay this parting compliment to his nephew. He expressed himself plainly about the folly of the Rands in "runnin' into debt for a shif'less fellow" who had no claim upon them. "If they expect me to pay the funeral expenses they're mistaken," he added, positively. "I ain't no call to do it, and I won't do it."

But he was not asked to defray the expenses of the simple funeral. It was paid for out of the minister's charitable fund.

"Some time I will pay you back the money, Mr. Morris," said Chester. "I am Mr. Bruce's heir, and it is right that I should pay."

"Very well, Chester. If your bequest amounts to anything I will not object. I hope for your sake that the lots may become valuable."

"I don't expect it, Mr. Morris. Will you be kind enough to take care of the papers for me?"

"Certainly, Chester. I will keep them with my own papers."

At this time Tacoma contained only four hundred inhabitants. The Northern Pacific Railroad had not been completed, and there was no certainty when it would be. So Chester did not pay much attention or give much thought to his Western property, but began to look round anxiously for something to do.

During the sickness of Walter Bruce he had given up his time to helping his mother and the care of the sick man. The money received from the minister enabled him to do this. Now the weekly income had ceased, and it became a serious question what he should do to bring in an income.

He had almost forgotten his meeting with Herbert Conrad, the young artist, when the day after the funeral he received a letter in an unknown hand, addressed to "Master Chester Rand, Wyncombe, New York."

As he opened it, his eyes opened wide with surprise and joy, when two five-dollar bills fluttered to the ground, for he had broken the seal in front of the post office.

He read the letter eagerly. It ran thus:

> "DEAR CHESTER:—I am glad to say that I have sold your sketch for ten dollars to one of the papers I showed you at Wyncombe. If you have any others ready, send them along. Try to think up some bright, original idea, and illustrate it in your best style. Then send to me.
>
> "Your sincere friend,
> HERBERT."

Chester hardly knew whether he was standing on his head or

his heels. It seems almost incredible that a sketch which he had dashed off in twenty minutes should bring in such a magnificent sum.

And for the first time it dawned upon him he was an artist. Fifty dollars gained in any other way would not have given him so much satisfaction. Why, it was only three weeks that he had been out of a place, and he had received more than he would have been paid in that time by Mr. Tripp.

He decided to tell no one of his good luck but his mother and the minister. If he were fortunate enough to earn more, the neighbors might wonder as they pleased about the source of his supplies. The money came at the right time, for his mother needed some articles at the store. He concluded to get them on the way home.

Silas Tripp was weighing out some sugar for a customer when Chester entered. Silas eyed him sharply, and was rather surprised to find him cheerful and in good spirits.

"How's your mother this mornin', Chester?" asked the grocer.

"Pretty well, thank you, Mr. Tripp."

"Are you doin' anything yet?"

"There doesn't seem to be much work to do in Wyncombe," answered Chester, noncommittally.

"You was foolish to leave a stiddy job at the store."

"I couldn't afford to work for the money you offered me."

"Two dollars and a quarter is better than nothin'. I would have paid you two and a half. I like you better than that

Wood boy. Is your mother workin'?"

"She is doing a little sewing, but she had no time for that with a sick man in the house."

"I don't see what made you keep a man that was no kith or kin to you."

"Would you have had us put him into the street, Mr. Tripp?"

"I'd have laid the matter before the selec'-men, and got him into the poorhouse."

"Well, it is all over now, and I'm not sorry that we cared for the poor fellow. I would like six pounds of sugar and two of butter."

"You ain't goin' to run a bill, be you?" asked Silas, cautiously. "I can't afford to trust out any more."

"We don't owe you anything, do we, Mr. Tripp?"

"No; but I thought mebbe—"

"I will pay for the articles," said Chester, briefly.

When he tendered the five-dollar bill Silas Tripp looked amazed.

"Where did you get so much money?" he gasped.

"Isn't it a good bill?" asked Chester.

"Why, yes, but—"

"I think that is all you have a right to ask," said Chester, firmly. "It can't make any difference to you where it came from."

"I thought you were poor," said Mr. Tripp.

"So we are."

"But it seems strange that you should have so much money."

"Five dollars isn't much money, Mr. Tripp."

Then a sudden idea came to Silas Tripp, and he paused in weighing out the butter.

"Did my nephew leave any money?" he asked, sharply.

"Yes, sir."

"Then I lay claim to it. I'm his only relation, and it is right that I should have it."

"You shall have it if you will pay the expense of his illness."

"Humph! how much did he leave?"

"Thirty-seven cents."

Mr. Tripp looked discomfited.

"You can keep it," he said, magnanimously. "I don't lay no claim to it."

"Thank you," returned Chester, gravely.

"Then this five-dollar bill didn't come from him?"

"How could it? he hadn't as much money in the world."

"He was a shif'less man. 'A rolling stone gathers no moss,'" observed Mr. Tripp, in a moralizing tone.

"You haven't been a rolling stone, Mr. Tripp."

"No; I've stuck to the store year in and year out for thirty-five years. I ain't had more'n three days off in that time."

"If I had your money, Mr. Tripp, I'd go off and enjoy myself."

"What, and leave the store?" said Silas, aghast at the thought.

"You could hire some one to run it."

"I wouldn't find much left when I came back; No, I must stay at home and attend to business. Do your folks go to bed early, Chester?"

"Not before ten," answered Chester, in some surprise.

"Then I'll call this evenin' after the store is closed."

"Very well, sir. You'll find us up."

The idea had occurred to Mr. Tripp that Mrs. Rand must be very short of money, and might be induced to dispose of her place at a largely reduced figure. It would be a good-paying investment for him, and he was not above taking advantage of a poor widow's necessities. Of course neither Mrs. Rand nor Chester had any idea of his motives or intentions, and they awaited his visit with considerable curiosity.

About fifteen minutes after nine a shuffling was heard at the door, there was a knock, and a minute later Chester admitted the thin and shriveled figure of Silas Tripp.

"Good-evening, Mr. Tripp," said Mrs. Rand, politely.

"Good-evenin', ma'am, I thought I'd call in and inquire how you were gettin' along."

"Thank you, Mr. Tripp, for the interest you show in our affairs. We are not doing very well, as you may imagine."

"So I surmised, ma'am. So I surmised."

"It can't be possible he is going to offer us a loan," thought Chester.

"You've got a tidy little place here, ma'am. It isn't mortgaged, I rec'on."

"No, Sir."

"Why don't you sell it? You need the money, and you might hire another house, or pay rent for this."

"Do you know of anyone that wants to buy it, Mr. Tripp?"

"Mebbe I'd buy it myself, jest to help you along," answered Silas, cautiously.

"How much would you be willing to give?" put in Chester.

"Well, I calculate—real estate's very low at present—three hundred and fifty dollars would be a fair price."

Mrs. Rand looked amazed.

"Three hundred and fifty dollars!" she ejaculated. "Why, it is worth at least seven hundred."

"You couldn't get it, ma'am. That's a fancy price."

"What rent would you charge in case we sold it to you, Mr. Tripp," asked Chester.

"Well, say five dollars a month."

"About sixteen or seventeen per cent. on the purchase money."

"Well, I'd have to pay taxes and repairs," explained Tripp.

"I don't care to sell, Mr. Tripp," said Mrs. Rand, decisively.

"You may have to, ma'am."

"If we do we shall try to get somewhere near its real value."

"Just as you like, ma'am," said Silas, disappointed. "I'd pay you cash down."

"If I decide to sell on your terms I'll let you know," said Mrs. Rand.

"Oh, well, I ain't set upon it. I only wanted to do you a favor."

"We appreciate your kindness," said Mrs. Rand, dryly.

"Women don't know much about business," muttered Silas, as he plodded home, disappointed.

CHAPTER VI

ROBERT RAMSAY

Mrs. Rand was as much amazed as Chester himself at his success as an artist.

"How long were you in making the drawing?" she asked.

"Twenty minutes."

"And you received ten dollars. It doesn't seem possible."

"I wish I could work twenty minutes every week at that rate," laughed Chester. "It would pay me better than working for Silas Tripp."

"Perhaps you can get some more work of the same kind?"

"I shall send two more sketches to Mr. Conrad in a day or two. I shall take pains and do my best."

Two days later Chester sent on the sketches, and then set about trying to find a job of some kind in the village. He heard of only one.

An elderly farmer, Job Dexter, offered him a dollar a week

and board if he would work for him. He would have eight cows to milk morning and night, the care of the barn, and a multitude of "chores" to attend to.

"How much will you give me if I board at home, Mr. Dexter?" asked Chester.

"I must have you in the house. I can't have you trapesing home when you ought to be at work."

"Then I don't think I can come, Mr. Dexter. A dollar a week wouldn't pay me."

"A dollar a week and board is good pay for a boy," said the farmer.

"It may be for some boys, but not for me."

Chester reflected that if he worked all day at the farmer's he could not do any artistic work, and so would lose much more than he made. The sketch sold by Mr. Conrad brought him in as much as he would receive in ten weeks from Farmer Dexter.

"Wyncombe people don't seem very liberal, mother," said Chester. "I thought Mr. Tripp pretty close, but Job Dexter beats him."

In the meantime he met Abel Wood carrying groceries to a family in the village.

"Have you got a place yet, Chester?" he asked.

"No; but I have a chance of one."

"Where?"

"At Farmer Dexter's."

"Don't you go! I worked for him once."

"How did you like it?"

"It almost killed me. I had to get up at half past four, work till seven in the evening, and all for a dollar a week and board."

"Was the board good?" inquired Chester, curiously.

"It was the poorest livin' I ever had. Mrs. Dexter don't know much about cookin'. We had baked beans for dinner three times a week, because they were cheap, and what was left was put on for breakfast the next mornin'."

"I like baked beans."

"You wouldn't like them as Mrs. Dexter cooked them, and you wouldn't want them for six meals a week."

"No, I don't think I should," said Chester, smiling. "How do you get along with Silas Tripp?"

"He's always scoldin'; he says I am not half as smart as you."

"I am much obliged to Mr. Tripp for his favorable opinion, but he didn't think enough of me to give me decent pay."

"He's awful mean. He's talkin' of reducin' me to two dollars a week. He says business is very poor, and he isn't makin' any money."

"I wish you and I were making half as much as he."

"There's one thing I don't understand, Chester. You ain't workin', yet you seem to have money."

"How do you know I have?"

"Mr. Tripp says you came into the store three or four days ago and changed a five-dollar bill."

"Yes; Mr. Tripp seemed anxious to know where I got it."

"You didn't use to have five-dollar bills, Chester, when you were at work."

"This five-dollar bill dropped down the chimney one fine morning," said Chester, laughing.

"I wish one would drop down my chimney. But I must be gettin' along, or old Tripp will give me hail Columbia when I get back."

About nine o'clock that evening, as Chester was returning from a lecture in the church, he was accosted by a rough-looking fellow having very much the appearance of a tramp, who seemed somewhat under the influence of liquor.

"I say, boss," said the tramp, "can't you give a poor man a quarter to help him along?"

"Are you out of work?" asked Chester, staying his step.

"Yes; times is hard and work is scarce. I haven't earned anything for a month."

"Where do you come from?"

"From Pittsburg," answered the tramp, with some hesitation.

"What do you work at when you are employed?"

"I am a machinist. Is there any chance in that line here?"

"Not in Wyncombe."

"That's what I thought. How about that quarter?"

"I am out of work myself and quarters are scarce with me."

"That's what you all say! There's small show for a good, industrious man."

Chester thought to himself that if the stranger was a good, industrious man he was unfortunate in his appearance.

"I have sympathy for all who are out of work," he said. "Mother and I are poor. When I did work I only got three dollars a week."

"Where did you work?"

"In Mr. Tripp's store, in the center of the village."

"I know. It's a two-story building, ain't it, with a piazza?"

"Yes."

"Has the old fellow got money?"

"Oh, yes; Silas Tripp is rich."

"So? He didn't pay you much wages, though."

"No; he feels poor. I dare say he feels poorer than I do."

"Such men ought not to have money," growled the tramp. "They're keepin' it out of the hands of honest men. What sort of a lookin' man is this man Tripp? Is he as big as me?"

"Oh, no, he is a thin, dried-up, little man, who looks as if he hadn't had a full meal of victuals in his life."

"What time does he shut up shop?"

"About this time," answered Chester, rather puzzled by the tramp's persistence in asking questions.

"What's your name?"

"Chester Rand."

"Can't you give me a quarter? I'm awful hungry. I ain't had a bit to eat since yesterday."

"I have no money to give you, but if you will come to our house I'll give you some supper."

"Where do you live?"

"About five minutes' walk."

"Go ahead, then; I'm with you."

Mrs. Rand looked up with surprise when the door opened and Chester entered, followed by an ill-looking tramp, whose clothes were redolent of tobacco, and his breath of whisky.

"Mother," said Chester, "this man tells me that he hasn't had anything to eat since yesterday."

"No more I haven't," spoke up the tramp, in a hoarse voice.

"He asked for some money. I could not give him that, but I told him we would give him some supper."

"Of course we will," said Mrs. Rand, in a tone of sympathy. She did not admire the appearance of her late visitor, but her heart was alive to the appeal of a hungry man.

"Sit down, sir," she said, "and I'll make some hot tea, and that with some bread and butter and cold meat will refresh you."

"Thank you, ma'am, I ain't overpartial to tea, and my doctor tells me I need whisky. You don't happen to have any whisky in the house, do you?"

"This is a temperance house," said Chester, "we never keep whisky."

"Well, maybe I can get along with the tea," sighed the tramp, in evident disappointment.

"You look strong and healthy," observed Mrs. Rand.

"I ain't, ma'am. Looks is very deceiving. I've got a weakness here," and he touched the pit of his stomach, "that calls for strengthenin' drink. But I'll be glad of the victuals."

When the table was spread with an extemporized supper, the unsavory visitor sat down, and did full justice to it. He even drank the tea, though he made up a face and called it "slops."

"Where did you come from, sir?" asked Mrs. Rand.

"From Chicago, ma'am."

"Were you at work there? What is your business?"

"I'm a blacksmith, ma'am."

"I thought you were a machinist and came from Pittsburg," interrupted Chester, in surprise.

"I came here by way of Pittsburg," answered the tramp, coughing. "I am machinist, too."

"His stories don't seem to hang together," thought Chester.

After supper the tramp, who said his name was Robert Ramsay, took out his pipe and began to smoke. If it had not been a cold evening, Mrs. Rand, who disliked tobacco, would have asked him to smoke out of doors, but as it was she tolerated it.

Both Chester and his mother feared that their unwelcome visitor would ask to stay all night, and they would not have felt safe with him in the house, but about a quarter past ten he got up and said he must be moving.

"Good-night, and good luck to you!" said Chester.

"Same to you!" returned the tramp.

"I wonder where he's going," thought Chester.

But when the next morning came he heard news that answered this question.

CHAPTER VII

SILAS TRIPP MAKES A DISCOVERY

When Silas Tripp went into his store the next day he was startled to find a window in the rear was partially open.

"How did that window come open, Abel?" he asked, as Abel Wood entered the store.

"I don't know, sir."

"It must have been you that opened it," said his employer, sternly.

"I didn't do it, Mr. Tripp, honest I didn't," declared Abel, earnestly.

"Then how did it come open, that's what I want to know?"

"I am sure I can't tell."

"Somebody might have come in during the night and robbed the store."

"So there might."

"It's very mysterious. Such things didn't happen when Chester was here."

Abel made no answer, but began to sweep out the store, his first morning duty.

When Silas spoke of the store being robbed he had no idea that such a robbing had taken place, but he went to the money drawer and opened it to make sure all was safe.

Instantly there was a cry of dismay.

"Abel!" he exclaimed, "I've been robbed. There's a lot of money missing."

Abel stopped sweeping and turned pale.

"Is that so, Mr. Tripp?" he asked, faintly.

"Yes, there's—lemme see. There's been burglars here. Oh, this is terrible!"

"Who could have done it, Mr. Tripp?"

"I dunno, but the store was entered last night. I never shall feel safe again," groaned Silas.

"Didn't they leave no traces?"

"Ha! here's a handkerchief," said Mr. Tripp, taking the article from the top of a flour barrel, "and yes, by gracious, it's marked Chester Rand."

"You don't think he took the money?" ejaculated Abel, in open-eyed wonder.

"Of course it must have been him! He knew just where I kept the money, and he could find his way about in the dark, he knew the store so well."

"I didn't think Chester would do such a thing."

"That's how he came by his five-dollar bill. He came in bold as brass and paid me with my own money—the young rascal!"

"But how could he do it if the money was took last night? It was two or three days ago he paid you the five-dollar bill."

This was a poser, but Mr. Tripp was equal to the emergency.

"He must have robbed me before," he said.

"You haven't missed money before, have you?"

"Not to my knowledge, but he must have took it. Abel, I want you to go right over to the Widow Rand's and tell Chester I want to see him. I dunno but I'd better send the constable after him."

"Shall I carry him his handkerchief?"

"No, and don't tell him it's been found. I don't want to put him on his guard."

Abel put his broom behind the door and betook himself to the house of Mrs. Rand.

The widow herself opened the door.

"Is Chester at home?" asked Abel.

"Yes, he's eating his breakfast. Do you want to see him?"

"Well, Mr. Tripp wants to see him."

"Possibly he wants Chester to give him a little extra help," she thought.

"Won't you come in and take a cup of coffee while Chester is finishing his breakfast?" she said.

"Thank you, ma'am."

Abel was a boy who was always ready to eat and drink, and he accepted the invitation with alacrity.

"So Mr. Tripp wants to see me?" said Chester. "Do you know what it's about?"

"He'll tell you," answered Abel, evasively.

Chester was not specially interested or excited. He finished his breakfast in a leisurely manner, and then taking his hat, went out with Abel. It occurred to him that Mr. Tripp might be intending to discharge Abel, and wished to see if he would return to his old place.

"So you don't know what he wants to see me about?" he asked.

"Well, I have an idea," answered Abel, in a mysterious tone.

"What is it, then?"

"Oh, I dassn't tell."

"Look here, Abel, I won't stir a step till you do tell me. You are acting very strangely."

"Well, somethin' terrible has happened," Abel ejaculated, in excited tones.

"What's it?"

"The store was robbed last night."

"The store was robbed?" repeated Chester. "What was taken?"

"Oh, lots and lots of money was taken from the drawer, and the window in the back of the store was left open."

"I'm sorry to hear it. I didn't know there was anybody in Wyncombe that would do such things. Does Mr. Tripp suspect anybody?"

"Yes, he does."

"Who is it?"

"He thinks you done it."

Chester stopped abruptly and looked amazed.

"Why, the man must be crazy! What on earth makes him think I would stoop to do such a thing?"

"'Cause your handkerchief was found on a flour barrel 'side of the money drawer."

"My handkerchief! Who says it was my handkerchief?"

"Your name was on it—in one corner; I seed it myself."

Then a light dawned upon Chester. The tramp whom he and his mother had entertained the evening before, must have picked up his handkerchief, and left it in the store to divert suspicion from himself. The detective instinct was born within Chester, and now he felt impatient to have the investigation proceed.

"Come on, Abel," he said, "I want to see about this matter."

"Well, you needn't walk so plaguy fast, wouldn't if I was you."

"Why not?"

"'Cause you'll probably have to go to jail. I'll tell you what I'd do."

"Well?"

"I'd hook it."

"You mean run away?"

"Yes."

"That's the last thing I'd do. Mr. Tripp would have a right to think I was guilty in that case."

"Well, ain't you?"

"Abel Wood, I have a great mind to give you a licking. Don't you know me any better than that?"

"Then why did you leave the handkerchief on the flour barrel?"

"That'll come out in due time."

They were near the store where Mr. Tripp was impatiently waiting for their appearance. He did not anticipate Abel's staying to breakfast, and his suspicions were excited.

"I'll bet Chester Rand has left town with the money," he groaned. "Oh, it's awful to have your hard earnin's carried off so sudden. I'll send Chester to jail unless he returns it—every cent of it."

Here Abel entered the store, followed by Chester.

CHAPTER VIII

A SCENE IN THE GROCERY STORE

"So you've come, have you, you young thief?" said Silas, sternly, as Chester entered the store. "Ain't you ashamed of yourself?"

"No, I'm not," Chester answered, boldly. "I've done nothing to be ashamed of."

"Oh, you hardened young villain. Give me the money right off, or I'll send you to jail."

"I hear from Abel that the store was robbed last night, and I suppose from what you say that you suspect me."

"So I do."

"Then you are mistaken. I spent all last night at home as my mother can testify."

"Then how came your handkerchief here?" demanded Silas, triumphantly, holding up the article.

"It must have been brought here."

"Oho, you admit that, do you? I didn't know but you'd say it came here itself."

"No, I don't think it did."

"I thought you'd own up arter a while."

"I own up to nothing."

"Isn't the handkerchief yours?"

"Yes."

"Then you stay here while Abel goes for the constable. You've got to be punished for such doin's. But I'll give ye one chance. Give me back the money you took—thirty-seven dollars and sixty cents—and I'll forgive ye, and won't have you sent to jail."

"That is a very kind offer, Mr. Tripp, and if I had taken the money I would accept it, and thank you. But I didn't take it."

"Go for the constable, Abel, and mind you hurry. You just stay where you are, Chester Rand. Don't you go for to run away."

Chester smiled. He felt that he had the key to the mystery, but he chose to defer throwing light upon it.

"On the way, Abel," said Chester, "please call at our house and ask my mother to come to the store."

"All right, Chester."

The constable was the first to arrive.

"What's wanted, Silas?" he asked, for in country villages neighbors are very apt to call one another by their Christian names.

"There's been robbery and burglary, Mr. Boody," responded Mr. Tripp. "My store was robbed last night of thirty-seven dollars and sixty cents."

"Sho, Silas, how you talk!"

"It's true, and there stands the thief!"

"I am sitting, Mr. Tripp," said Chester smiling.

"See how he brazens it out! What a hardened young villain he is!"

"Come, Silas, you must be crazy," expostulated the constable, who felt very friendly to Chester. "Chester wouldn't no more steal from you than I would."

"I thought so myself, but when I found his handkerchief, marked with his name, on a flour barrel, I was convinced."

"Is that so, Chester?"

"Yes, the handkerchief is mine."

"It wasn't here last night," proceeded Silas, "and it was here this morning. It stands to reason that it couldn't have walked here itself, and so of course it was brought here."

By this time two other villagers entered the store.

"What do you say to that, Chester?" said the constable, beginning to be shaken in his conviction of Chester's innocence.

"I agree with Mr. Tripp. It must have been brought here."

At this moment, Mrs. Rand and the minister whom she had met on the way, entered the store.

"Glad to see you, widder," said Silas Tripp, grimly. "I hope you ain't a-goin' to stand up for your son in his didoes."

"I shall certainly stand by Chester, Mr. Tripp. What is the trouble?"

"Only that he came into my store in the silent watches of last night," answered Silas, sarcastically, "and made off with thirty-seven dollars and sixty cents."

"It's a falsehood, whoever says it," exclaimed Mrs. Rand, hotly.

"I supposed you'd stand up for him," sneered Silas.

"And for a very good reason. During the silent watches of last night, as you express it, Chester was at home and in bed to my certain knowledge."

"While his handkerchief walked over here and robbed the store," suggested Silas Tripp, with withering sarcasm, as he held up the telltale evidence of Chester's dishonesty.

"Was this handkerchief found in the store?" asked Mrs. Rand, in surprise.

"Yes, ma'am, it was, and I calculate you'll find it hard to get over that evidence."

Mrs. Rand's face lighted up with a sudden conviction.

"I think I can explain it," she said, quietly.

"Oh, you can, can you? Maybe you can tell who took the money."

"I think I can."

All eyes were turned upon her in eager expectation.

"A tramp called at our house last evening," she said, "at about half-past nine, and I gave him a meal, as he professed to be hungry and penniless. It was some minutes after ten when he left the house. He must have picked up Chester's handkerchief, and left it in your store after robbing the money drawer."

"That's all very fine," said Silas, incredulously, "but I don't know as there was any tramp. Nobody saw him but you."

"I beg your pardon, Mr. Tripp," said the minister, "but I saw him about half-past ten walking in the direction of your store. I was returning from visiting a sick parishioner when I met a man roughly dressed and of middle height, walking up the street. He was smoking a pipe."

"He lighted it before leaving our house," said Mrs. Rand.

"How did he know about my store?" demanded Silas, incredulously.

"He was asking questions about you while he was eating his supper."

Silas Tripp was forced to confess, though reluctantly, that the case against Chester was falling to the ground. But he did not like to give up.

"I'd like to know where Chester got the money he's been flauntin' round the last week," he said.

"Probably he stole it from your store last night," said the constable, with good-natured sarcasm.

"That ain't answerin' the question."

"I don't propose to answer the question," said Chester, firmly. "Where I got my money is no concern of Mr. Tripp, as long as I don't get it from him."

"Have I got to lose the money?" asked Silas, in a tragical tone. "It's very hard on a poor man."

All present smiled, for Silas was one of the richest men in the village.

"We might take up a contribution for you, Silas," said the constable, jocosely.

"Oh, it's all very well for you to joke about it, considerin' you didn't lose it."

At this moment Abel Wood, who had been sweeping the piazza, entered the store in excitement.

"I say, there's the tramp now," he exclaimed.

"Where? Where?" asked one and another.

"Out in the street. Constable Perkins has got him."

"Call him in," said the minister.

A moment later, Constable Perkins came in, escorting the

tramp, who was evidently under the influence of strong potations, and had difficulty in holding himself up.

"Where am I?" hiccoughed Ramsay.

"Where did you find him, Mr. Perkins?" asked Rev. Mr. Morris.

"Just outside of Farmer Dexter's barn. He was lying on the ground, with a jug of whisky at his side."

"It was my jug," said Silas. "He must have taken it from the store. I didn't miss it before. He must have took it away with him."

"There warn't much whisky left in the jug. He must have absorbed most of it."

Now Mr. Tripp's indignation was turned against this new individual.

"Where is my money, you villain?" he demanded, hotly.

"Whaz-zer matter?" hiccoughed Ramsay.

"You came into my store last night and stole some money."

"Is zis zer store? It was jolly fun," and the inebriate laughed.

"Yes, it is. Where is the money you took?"

"Spent it for whisky."

"No, you didn't. You found the whisky here."

Ramsay made no reply.

"He must have the money about him," suggested the minister. "You'd better search his pockets, Mr. Perkins."

The constable thrust his hand into the pocket of his helpless charge, and drew out a roll of bills.

Silas Tripp uttered an exclamation of joy.

"Give it to me," he said. "It's my money."

The bills were counted and all were there.

Not one was missing. Part of the silver could not be found. It had probably slipped from his pocket, for he had no opportunity of spending any.

Mr. Tripp was so pleased to recover his bills that he neglected to complain of the silver coins that were missing. But still he felt incensed against the thief.

"You'll suffer for this," he said, sternly, eying the tramp over his glasses.

"Who says I will?"

"I say so. You'll have to go to jail."

"I'm a 'spectable man," hiccoughed the tramp. "I'm an honest man. I ain't done nothin'."

"Why did you take my handkerchief last night?" asked Chester.

The tramp laughed.

"Good joke, wasn't it? So they'd think it was you."

"It came near being a bad joke for me. Do you think I robbed your store now, Mr. Tripp?"

To this question Silas Tripp did not find it convenient to make an answer. He was one of those men—very numerous they are, too—who dislike to own themselves mistaken.

"It seems to me, Mr. Tripp," said the minister, "that you owe an apology to our young friend here for your false suspicions."

"Anybody'd suspect him when they found his handkerchief," growled Silas.

"But now you know he was not concerned in the robbery you should make reparation."

"I don't know where he got his money," said Silas. "There's suthin' very mysterious about that five-dollar bill."

"I've got another, Mr. Tripp," said Chester, smiling.

"Like as not. Where'd you get it?"

"I don't feel obliged to tell."

"It looks bad, that's all I've got to say," said the storekeeper.

"I think, Mr. Tripp, you need not borrow any trouble on that score," interposed the minister. "I know where Chester's money comes from, and I can assure you that it is honestly earned, more so than that which you receive from the whisky you sell."

Silas Tripp was a little afraid of the minister, who was very plain-spoken, and turned away muttering.

The crowd dispersed, some following Constable Perkins, who took his prisoner to the lockup.

Horatio Alger, Jr

CHAPTER IX

NEW PLANS FOR CHESTER

Two days later Chester found another letter from Mr. Conrad at the post office. In it were two bills—a ten and a five.

Mr. Conrad wrote:

"I have disposed of your two sketches to the same paper. The publisher offered me fifteen dollars for the two, and I thought it best to accept. Have you ever thought of coming to New York to live? You would be more favorably placed for disposing of your sketches, and would find more subjects in a large city than in a small village. The fear is that, if you continue to live in Wyncombe, you will exhaust your invention.

"There is one objection, the precarious nature of the business. You might sometimes go a month, perhaps, without selling a sketch, and meanwhile your expenses would go on. I think, however, that I have found a way of obviating this objection. I have a friend—Mr. Bushnell— who is in the real estate business, and he will take you into his office on my recommendation. He will pay you five dollars a week if he finds you satisfactory. This will afford you a steady income, which you can supplement by your art work. If you decide to accept my suggestion come to New York next Saturday, and you can stay with me over Sunday, and go to work on Monday morning.

"Your sincere friend,

"HERBERT CONRAD."

Chester read this letter in a tumult of excitement. The great city had always had a fascination for him, and he had hoped, without much expectation of the hope being realized, that he might one day find employment there. Now the opportunity had come, but could he accept it? The question arose, How would his mother get along in his absence? She would be almost entirely without income. Could he send her enough from the city to help her along?

He went to his mother and showed her the letter.

"Fifteen dollars!" she exclaimed. "Why, that is fine, Chester. I shall begin to be proud of you. Indeed, I am proud of you now."

"I can hardly realize it myself, mother. I won't get too much elated, for it may not last. What do you think of Mr. Conrad's proposal?"

"To go to New York?"

"Yes."

Mrs. Rand's countenance fell.

"I don't see how I can spare you, Chester," she said, soberly.

"If there were any chance of making a living in Wyncombe,

it would be different."

"You might go back to Mr. Tripp's store."

"After he had charged me with stealing? No, mother, I will never serve Silas Tripp again."

"There might be some other chance."

"But there isn't, mother. By the way, I heard at the post office that the shoe manufactory will open again in three weeks."

"That's good news. I shall have some more binding to do."

"And I can send you something every week from New York."

"But I will be so lonely, Chester, with no one else in the house."

"That is true, mother."

"But I won't let that stand in the way. You may have prospects in New York. You have none here."

"And, as Mr. Conrad says, I am likely to run out of subjects for sketches."

"I think I shall have to give my consent, then."

"Thank you, mother," said Chester, joyfully. "I will do what I can to pay you for the sacrifice you are making."

Just then the doorbell rang.

"It is Mr. Gardener, the lawyer," said Chester, looking from the window.

A moment later he admitted the lawyer.

"Well, Chester," said Mr. Gardener, pleasantly, "have you disposed of your lots in Tacoma yet?"

"No, Mr. Gardener. In fact, I had almost forgotten about them."

"Sometime they may prove valuable."

"I wish it might be soon."

"I fancy you will have to wait a few years. By the time you are twenty-one you may come into a competence."

"I won't think of it till then."

"That's right. Work as if you had nothing to look forward to."

"You don't want to take me into your office and make a lawyer of me, Mr. Gardener, do you?"

"Law in Wyncombe does not offer any inducements. If I depended on my law business, I should fare poorly, but thanks to a frugal and industrious father, I have a fair income outside of my earnings. Mrs. Rand, my visit this morning is to you. How would you like to take a boarder?"

Chester and his mother looked surprised.

"Who is it, Mr. Gardener?"

"I have a cousin, a lady of forty, who thinks of settling down in Wyncombe. She thinks country air will be more favorable to her health than the city."

"Probably she is used to better accommodations than she would find here."

"My cousin will be satisfied with a modest home."

"We have but two chambers, mine and Chester's."

"But you know, mother, I am going to New York to work."

"That's true; your room will be vacant."

Mr. Gardener looked surprised.

"Isn't this something new," he asked, "about you going to New York, I mean?"

"Yes, sir; that letter from Mr. Conrad will explain all."

Mr. Gardener read the letter attentively.

"I think the plan a good one," he said. "You will find that you will work better in a great city. Then, if my cousin comes, your mother will not be so lonesome."

"It is the very thing," said Chester, enthusiastically.

"What is your cousin's name, Mr. Gardener?" asked the widow.

"Miss Jane Dolby. She is a spinster, and at her age there is not much chance of her changing her condition. Shall I write her that you will receive her?"

"Yes; I shall be glad to do so."

"And, as Miss Dolby is a business woman, she will expect me to tell her your terms."

"Will four dollars a week be too much?" asked Mrs. Rand, in a tone of hesitation.

"Four dollars, my dear madam!"

"Do you consider it too much? I am afraid I could not afford to say less."

"I consider it too little. My cousin is a woman of means. I will tell her your terms are eight dollars a week including washing."

"But will she be willing to pay so much?"

"She pays twelve dollars a week in the city, and could afford to pay more. She is not mean, but is always willing to pay a good price."

"I can manage very comfortably on that sum," said Mrs. Rand, brightening up. "I hope I shall be able to make your cousin comfortable."

"I am sure of it. Miss Dolby is a very sociable lady, and if you are willing to hear her talk she will be content."

"She will keep me from feeling lonesome."

When Mr. Gardener left the house, Chester said: "All things seem to be working in aid of my plans, mother, I feel much more comfortable now that you will have company."

"Besides, Chester, you will not need to send me any money. The money Miss Dolby pays me will be sufficient to defray the expenses of the table, and I shall still have some time for binding shoes."

"Then I hope I may be able to save some money."

During the afternoon Chester went to the store to buy groceries. Mr. Tripp himself filled the order. He seemed disposed to be friendly.

"Your money holds out well, Chester," he said, as he made change for a two-dollar bill.

"Yes, Mr. Tripp."

"I can't understand it, for my part. Your mother must be a good manager."

"Yes, Mr. Tripp, she is."

"You'd orter come back to work for me, Chester."

"But you have got a boy already."

"The Wood boy ain't worth shucks. He ain't got no push, and he's allus forgettin' his errands. If you'll come next Monday I'll pay you two dollars and a half a week. That's pooty good for these times."

"I'm sorry to disappoint you, Mr. Tripp, but I am going to work somewhere else."

"Where?" asked Silas, in great surprise.

"In New York," answered Chester, proudly.

"You don't say! How'd you get it?"

"Mr. Conrad, an artist, a friend of the minister, got it for me."

"Is your mother willin' to have you go?"

"She will miss me, but she thinks it will be for my advantage."

"How's she goin' to live? It will take all you can earn to pay your own way in a big city. In fact, I don't believe you can do it."

"I'll try, Mr. Tripp."

Chester did not care to mention the new boarder that was expected, as he thought it probable that Mr. Tripp, who always looked out for his own interests, would try to induce Miss Dolby to board with him. As Mr. Tripp had the reputation of keeping a very poor table, he had never succeeded in retaining a boarder over four weeks.

Chester found that his clothing needed replenishing, and ventured to spend five dollars for small articles, such as handkerchiefs, socks, etc. Saturday morning he walked to the depot with a small gripsack in his hand and bought a ticket for New York.

CHAPTER X

A RAILROAD ACQUAINTANCE

The distance by rail from Wyncombe to New York is fifty miles. When about eight years of age Chester had made the journey, but not since then. Everything was new to him, and, of course, interesting. His attention was drawn from the scenery by the passage of a train boy through the cars with a bundle of new magazines and papers.

"Here is all the magazines, *Puck* and *Judge*."

"How much do you charge for *Puck*?" asked Chester, with interest, for it was *Puck* that had accepted his first sketch.

"Ten cents."

"Give me one."

Chester took the paper and handed the train boy a dime.

Then he began to look over the pages. All at once he gave a start, his face flushed, his heart beat with excitement. There was his sketch looking much more attractive on the fair pages of the periodical than it had done in his pencil drawing. He kept looking at it. It seemed to have a fascination for him. It was his first appearance in a paper, and it was a proud moment for him.

"What are you looking at so intently, my son?" asked the gentleman who sat at his side. He was a man of perhaps middle age, and he wore spectacles, which gave him a literary aspect.

"I—I am looking at this sketch," answered Chester, in slight confusion.

"Let me see it."

Chester handed over the paper and regarded his seat mate with some anxiety. He wanted to see what impression this, his maiden effort, would have on a staid man of middle age.

"Ha! very good!" said his companion, "but I don't see anything very remarkable about it. Yet you were looking at it for as much as five minutes."

"Because it is mine," said Chester, half proudly, half in embarrassment.

"Ah! that is different. Did you really design it?"

"Yes, sir."

"I suppose you got pay for it. I understand *Puck* pays for everything it publishes."

"Yes, sir; I got ten dollars."

"Ten dollars!" repeated the gentleman, in surprise. "Really that is very handsome. Do you often produce such sketches?"

"I have just begun, sir. That is the first I have had published."

"You are beginning young. How old are you?"

"I am almost sixteen."

"That is young for an artist. Why, I am forty-five, and I haven't a particle of talent in that direction. My youngest son asked me the other day to draw a cow on the slate. I did as well as I could, and what do you think he said?"

"What did he say?" asked Chester, interested.

"He said, 'Papa, if it wasn't for the horns I should think it was a horse.'"

Chester laughed. It was a joke he could appreciate.

"I suppose all cannot draw," he said.

"It seems not. May I ask you if you live in New York—the city, I mean?"

"No, sir."

"But you are going there?"

"Yes, sir."

"To live?"

"I hope so. A friend has written advising me to come. He says I will be better placed to do art work, and dispose of my sketches."

"Are you expecting to earn your living that way?"

"I hope to some time, but not at first."

"I am glad to hear it. I should think you would find it very precarious."

"I expect to work in a real estate office at five dollars a week, and only to spend my leisure hours in art work."

"That seems sensible. Have you been living in the country?"

"Yes, sir, in Wyncombe."

"I have heard of the place, but was never there. So you are just beginning the battle of life?"

"Yes, sir."

"It has just occurred to me that I may be able to throw some work in your way. I am writing an ethnological work, and it will need to be illustrated. I can't afford to pay such prices as you receive from *Puck* and other periodicals of the same class, but then the work will not be original. It will consist chiefly of copies. I should think I might need a hundred illustrations, and I am afraid I could not pay more than two dollars each."

A hundred illustrations at two dollars each! Why, that would amount to two hundred dollars, and there would be no racking his brains for original ideas.

"If you think I can do the work, sir, I shall be glad to undertake it," said Chester, eagerly.

"I have no doubt you can do it, for it will not require an expert. Suppose you call upon me some evening within a week."

"I will do so gladly, sir, if you will tell me where you live."

"Here is my card," said his companion, drawing out his case, and handing a card to Chester.

This was what Chester read:

"Prof. Edgar Hazlitt."

"Do you know where Lexington Avenue is?" asked the professor.

"I know very little about New York. In fact, nothing at all," Chester was obliged to confess.

"You will soon find your way about. I have no doubt you will find me," and the professor mentioned the number. "Shall we say next Wednesday evening, at eight o'clock sharp? That's if you have no engagement for that evening," he added, with a smile.

Chester laughed at the idea of his having any evening engagements in a city which he had not seen for eight years.

"If you are engaged to dine with William Vanderbilt or Jay Gould on that evening," continued the professor, with a merry look, "I will say Thursday."

"If I find I am engaged in either place, I think I can get off," said Chester.

"Then Wednesday evening let it be!"

As the train neared New York Chester began to be solicitous about finding Mr. Conrad in waiting for him. He knew nothing about the city, and would feel quite helpless should the artist not be present to meet him. He left the car and walked slowly along the platform, looking eagerly on all sides for the expected friendly face.

But nowhere could he see Herbert Conrad.

In some agitation he took from his pocket the card containing his friend's address, and he could hardly help inwardly reproaching him for leaving an inexperienced boy in the lurch. He was already beginning to feel homesick and forlorn, when a bright-looking lad of twelve, with light-brown hair, came up and asked: "Is this Chester Rand?"

"Yes," answered Chester, in surprise. "How do you know my name?"

"I was sent here by Mr. Conrad to meet you."

Chester brightened up at once. So his friend had not forgotten him after all.

"Mr. Conrad couldn't come to meet you, as he had an important engagement, so he sent me to bring you to his room. I am Rob Fisher."

"I suppose that means Robert Fisher?"

"Yes, but everybody calls me Rob."

"Are you a relation of Mr. Conrad?"

"Yes, I am his cousin. I live just outside of the city, but I am visiting my cousin for the day. I suppose you don't know much about New York?"

"I know nothing at all."

"I am pretty well posted, and I come into the city pretty often. Just follow me. Shall I carry your valise?"

"Oh, no; I am older than you and better able to carry it. What street is this?"

"Forty-second Street. We will go to Fifth Avenue, and then walk down to Thirty-fourth Street."

"That is where Mr. Conrad lives, isn't it?"

"Yes; it is one of the wide streets, like Fourteenth and Twenty-third, and this street."

"There are some fine houses here."

"I should think so. You live in Wyncombe, don't you?"

"Yes; the houses are all of wood there."

"I suppose so. Mr. Conrad tells me you are an artist," said Rob, eying his new friend with curiosity.

"In a small way."

"I should like to see some of your pictures."

"I can show you one," and Chester opened his copy of *Puck* and pointed to the sketch already referred to.

"Did you really draw this yourself?"

"Yes."

"And did you get any money for it?"

"Ten dollars," answered Chester, with natural pride.

"My! I wish I could get money for drawing."

"Perhaps you can some time."

Bob shook his head.

"I haven't any talent that way."

"What house is that?" asked Chester, pointing to the marble mansion at the corner of Thirty-fourth Street.

"That used to belong to A. T. Stewart, the great merchant. I suppose you haven't any houses like that in Wyncombe?"

"Oh, no."

"We will turn down here. This is Thirty-fourth Street."

They kept on, crossing Sixth and Seventh Avenues, and presently stood in front of a neat, brownstone house between Seventh and Eighth Avenues.

"That is where Mr. Conrad lives," said Rob.

CHAPTER XI

CHESTER'S FIRST EXPERIENCES IN NEW YORK

The bell was rung, and a servant opened the door.

"I will go up to Mr. Conrad's room," said Rob.

The servant knew him, and no objection was made. They went up two flights to the front room on the third floor. Rob opened the door without ceremony and entered, followed by Chester.

He found himself in a spacious room, neatly furnished and hung around with engravings, with here and there an oil painting. There was a table near the window with a portfolio on it. Here, no doubt, Mr. Conrad did some of his work. There was no bed in the room, but through an open door Chester saw a connecting bedroom.

"This is a nice room," he said.

"Yes, cousin Herbert likes to be comfortable. Here, give me your valise, and make yourself at home."

Chester sat down by the window and gazed out on the broad street. It was a pleasant, sunny day, and everything looked bright and attractive.

"You are going to live in New York, aren't you?" asked Rob.

"Yes, if I can make a living here."

"I guess cousin Herbert will help you."

"He has already. He has obtained a place for me in a real estate office at five dollars a week."

"I think I could live on five dollars a week."

"I suppose it costs considerable to live in New York."

Chester felt no apprehension, however. He was sure he should succeed, and, indeed, he had reason to feel encouraged, for had he not already engaged two hundred dollars' worth of work?—and this sum seemed as much to him as two thousand would have done to Mr. Conrad.

An hour glided by rapidly, and then a step was heard on the stairs.

"That's cousin Herbert," said Rob, and he ran to open the door.

"Hello, Rob. Did you find Chester?"

"Yes, here he is!"

"Glad to see you, Chester," said the artist, shaking his hand cordially; "you must excuse my not going to meet you, but I was busily engaged on a large drawing for *Harper's Weekly*, and, feeling in a favorable mood, I didn't want to lose the benefit of my inspiration. You will find when you have more experience that an artist can accomplish three times as much when in the mood.

"I am glad you didn't leave off for me. Rob has taken good care of me."

"Yes, Rob is used to the city; I thought you would be in safe hands. And how do you like my quarters?"

"They are very pleasant. And the street is so wide, too."

"Yes, I like Thirty-fourth street. I lodge, but I don't board here."

Chester was surprised to hear this. In Wyncombe everyone took his meals in the same house in which he lodged.

"And that reminds me, don't you feel hungry? I don't ask Rob, for he always has an appetite. How is it with you, Chester?"

"I took a very early breakfast."

"So I thought," laughed Conrad. "Well, put on our coats, and we'll go to Trainor's."

They walked over to Sixth Avenue and entered a restaurant adjoining the Standard Theater. It was handsomely decorated, and seemed to Chester quite the finest room he was ever in. Ranged in three rows were small tables, each designed for four persons. One of these was vacant, and Conrad took a seat on one side, placing the two boys opposite.

"Now," he said, "I had better do the ordering. We will each order a different dish, and by sharing them we will have a variety."

There is no need to mention of what the dinner consisted. All three enjoyed it, particularly the two boys. It was the first meal Chester had taken in a restaurant, and he could not get rid of a feeling of embarrassment at the thought that the waiters, who were better dressed than many of the prominent citizens of Wyncombe, were watching him. He did not, however, allow this feeling to interfere with his appetite.

"Do you always eat here, Mr. Conrad?" asked Chester.

"No; sometimes it is more convenient to go elsewhere. Now and then I take a table d'hote dinner."

"I don't think I can afford to come here often," Chester remarked, after consulting the bill of fare and the prices set down opposite the different dishes.

"No; it will be better for you to secure a boarding place. You want to be economical for the present. How did you leave your mother?"

"Very well, thank you, Mr. Conrad. We have been very fortunate in securing a boarder who pays eight dollars a week, so that mother thinks she can get along for the present without help from me."

"That is famous. Where did you get such a boarder in Wyncombe?"

"It is a lady, the cousin of Mr. Gardener, the lawyer. She will be company for mother."

"It is an excellent arrangement. Now, boys, if you have finished, I will go up and settle the bill."

As they left the restaurant, Mr. Conrad said:

Horatio Alger, Jr

"In honor of your arrival, I shall not work any more to-day. Now, shall we go back to my room, or would you like to take a walk and see something of the city?"

The unanimous decision was for the stroll.

Mr. Conrad walked down Broadway with the boys, pointing out any notable buildings on the way. Chester was dazzled. The great city exceeded his anticipations. Everything seemed on so grand a scale to the country boy, and with his joyous excitement there mingled the thought: "And I, too, am going to live here. I shall have a share in the great city, and mingle in its scenes every day."

Rob was used to the city, and took matters quietly. He was not particularly impressed. Yet he could not help enjoying the walk, so perfect was the weather. As they passed Lord & Taylor's, a lady came out of the store.

"Why, mother," said Rob, "is that you?"

"Yes, Rob. I came in on a shopping excursion, and I want you to go with me and take care of me."

Rob grumbled a little, but, of course, acceded to his mother's request. So Chester was left alone with Mr. Conrad.

"How do you feel about coming to New York, Chester?" asked his friend. "You are not afraid of failure, are you?"

"No, Mr. Conrad, I feel very hopeful. Something has happened to me to-day that encourages me very much."

"What is it?"

Chester told the story of his meeting with Prof. Hazlitt, and the proposition which had been made to him.

"Why, this is famous," exclaimed Conrad, looking pleased. "I know of Prof. Hazlitt, though I never met him. He was once professor in a Western college, but inheriting a fortune from his uncle, came to New York to pursue his favorite studies. He does not teach now, but, I believe, delivers an annual course of lectures before the students of Columbia College. He is a shrewd man, and the offer of employment from him is indeed a compliment. I am very glad you met him. He may throw other work in your way."

"I hope I can give him satisfaction," said Chester. "It makes me feel rich whenever I think of the sum I am to receive. Two hundred dollars is a good deal of money."

"To a boy like you, yes. It doesn't go very far with me now. It costs a good deal for me to live. How much do you think I have to pay for my room—without board?"

"Three dollars a week," guessed Chester.

Mr. Conrad smiled.

"I pay ten dollars a week," he said.

Chester's breath was quite taken away.

"Why, I did not think the whole house would cost as much—for rent."

"You will get a more correct idea of New York expenses after a while. Now, let me come back to your plans. You had better stay with me for a few days."

"But I am afraid I shall be putting you to inconvenience,

Mr. Conrad."

"No; it will be pleasant for me to have your company. On Monday morning I will go with you to the office of the real estate broker who is to employ you."

Chester passed Sunday pleasantly, going to church in the forenoon, and taking a walk with Mr. Conrad in the afternoon. He wrote a short letter to his mother, informing her of his safe arrival in the city, but not mentioning his engagement by Prof. Hazlitt. He preferred to wait till he had an interview with the professor, and decided whether he could do the work satisfactorily.

"Your future employer is Clement Fairchild," said the artist. "His office is on West Fourteenth Street, between Seventh and Eight Avenues."

"What sort of a man is he?" asked Chester.

"I don't know him very well, but I believe he does a very good business. You will know more about him in a week than I can tell you. There is one comfort, and that is that you are not wholly dependent upon him. I advise you, however, to say nothing in the office about your art work. Business men sometimes have a prejudice against outside workers. They feel that an employee ought to be solely occupied with their interests."

"I will remember what you say, Mr. Conrad."

Chester looked forward with considerable curiosity and some anxiety to his coming interview with Mr. Fairchild.

CHAPTER XII

A REAL ESTATE OFFICE

About eight o'clock on Monday morning Chester, accompanied by his friend Conrad, turned down Fourteenth Street from Sixth Avenue and kept on till they reached an office over which was the sign:

"Clement Fairchild, Real Estate."

"This is the place, Chester," said the artist. "I will go in and introduce you."

They entered the office. It was of fair size, and contained a high desk, an office table covered with papers, and several chairs. There was but one person in the office, a young man with black whiskers and mustache and an unamiable expression. He sat on a high stool, but he was only reading the morning paper. He turned lazily as he heard the door open, and let his glance rest on Mr. Conrad.

"What can I do for you?" he asked, in a careless tone.

"Is Mr. Fairchild in?" asked the artist.

"No."

"When will he be in?"

"Can't say, I am sure. If you have any business, I will attend to it."

"I have no special business, except to introduce my young friend here."

"Indeed!" said the clerk, impudently. "Who is he?"

"He is going to work here," returned Mr. Conrad, sharply.

"What?" queried the bookkeeper, evidently taken by surprise. "Who says he is going to work here?"

"Mr. Fairchild."

"He didn't say anything to me about it."

"Very remarkable, certainly," rejoined Conrad. "I presume you have no objection."

"Look here," said the bookkeeper, "I think there is some mistake about this. The place was all but promised to my cousin."

"You'll have to settle that matter with your employer. Apparently he doesn't tell you everything, Mr. —"

"My name is Mullins—David Mullins," said the bookkeeper, with dignity.

"Then, Mr. Mullins, I have the pleasure of introducing to you Chester Rand, late of Wyncombe, now of New York, who will be associated with you in the real estate business."

"Perhaps so," sneered Mullins.

"He will stay here till Mr. Fairchild makes his appearance."

"Oh, he can sit down if he wants to."

"I shall have to leave you, Chester, as I must get to work. When Mr. Fairchild comes in, show him this note from me."

"All right, sir."

Chester was rather chilled by his reception. He saw instinctively that his relations with Mr. Mullins were not likely to be cordial, and he suspected that if the bookkeeper could get him into trouble he would.

After the artist had left the office, Mr. David Mullins leisurely picked his teeth with his pen-knife, and fixed a scrutinizing glance on Chester, of whom he was evidently taking the measure.

"Do you knew Mr. Fairchild?" he at length asked, abruptly.

"No, sir."

"It's queer he should have engaged you as office boy."

Chester did not think it necessary to make any reply to this remark.

"How much salary do you expect to get?"

"Five dollars a week."

"Who told you so?"

"The gentleman who came in with me."

"Who is he?"

"Mr. Herbert Conrad, an artist and draughtsman."

"Never heard of him."

Mr. Mullins spoke as if this was enough to settle the status of Mr. Conrad. A man whom he did not know must be obscure.

"So, Mr. Fairchild engaged you through Mr. Conrad, did he?"

"Yes, sir."

"Do you know anything about the city?"

"Not much."

"Then I can't imagine why Mr. Fairchild should have hired you. You can't be of much use here."

Chester began to feel discouraged. All this was certainly very depressing.

"I shall try to make myself useful," he said.

"Oh, yes," sneered Mr. Mullins, "new boys always say that."

There was a railing stretching across the office about midway, dividing it into two parts. The table and desk were inside. The remaining space was left for the outside public.

A poor woman entered the office, her face bearing the impress of sorrow.

"Is Mr. Fairchild in?" she asked.

"No, he isn't."

"I've come in about the month's rent."

"Very well! You can pay it to me. What name?"

"Mrs. Carlin, sir."

"Ha! yes. Your rent is six dollars. Pass it over, and I will give you a receipt."

"But I came to say that I had only three dollars and a half toward it."

"And why have you only three dollars and a half, I'd like to know?" said Mullins, rudely.

"Because my Jimmy has been sick three days. He's a telegraph boy, and I'm a widow, wid only me bye to help me."

"I have nothing to do with the sickness of your son. When you hired your rooms, you agreed to pay the rent, didn't you?"

"Yes, sir; but—"

"And you didn't say anything about Jimmy being sick or well."

"True for you, sir; but—"

"I think, Mrs. Carlin, you'll have to get hold of the other two dollars and a half some how, or out you'll go. See?"

"Shure, sir, you are very hard with a poor widow," said Mrs. Carlin, wiping her eyes with the corner of her apron.

"Business is business, Mrs. Carlin."

"If Mr. Fairchild were in, he'd trate me better than you. Will he be in soon?"

"Perhaps he will, and perhaps he won't. You can pay the money to me."

"I won't, sir, beggin' your pardon. I'd rather wait and see him."

"Very well! you can take the consequences," and Mr. Mullins eyed the widow with an unpleasant and threatening glance.

She looked very sad, and Chester felt that he should like to give the bookkeeper a good shaking. He could not help despising a man who appeared to enjoy distressing an unfortunate woman whose only crime was poverty.

At this moment the office door opened, and a gentleman of perhaps forty entered. He was a man with a kindly face, and looked far less important than the bookkeeper. Mr. Mullins, on seeing him, laid aside his unpleasant manner, and said, in a matter-of-fact tone:

"This is Mrs. Carlin. She owes six dollars rent, and only brings three dollars and a half."

"How is this, Mrs. Carlin?" inquired Mr. Fairchild, for this was he.

Mrs. Carlin repeated her story of Jimmy's illness and her

consequent inability to pay the whole rent.

"When do you think Jimmy will get well?" asked the agent, kindly.

"He's gettin' better fast, sir. I think he'll be able to go to work by Wednesday. If you'll only wait a little while, sir—"

"How long have you been paying rent here?" asked Mr. Fairchild.

"This is the third year, sir."

"And have you ever been in arrears before?"

"No, sir."

"Then you deserve consideration. Mr. Mullins, give Mrs. Carlin a receipt on account, and she will pay the balance as soon as she can."

"Thank you, sir. May the saints reward you, sir! Shure, I told this gentleman that you'd make it all right with me. He was very hard with me."

"Mr. Mullins," said the agent, sternly, "I have before now told you that our customers are to be treated with consideration and kindness."

David Mullins did not reply, but he dug his pen viciously into the paper on which he was writing a receipt, and scowled, but as his back was turned to his employer, the latter did not see it.

When Mrs. Carlin had left the office, Chester thought it best to introduce himself.

"I am Chester Rand, from Wyncombe," he said. "Mr. Conrad came round to introduce me, but you were not in."

"Ah, yes, you have come to be my office boy. I am glad to see you and hope you will like the city. Mr. Mullins, you will set this boy to work."

"He told me he was to work here, but as you had not mentioned it I thought there must be some mistake. He says he doesn't know much about the city."

"Neither did I when I first came here from a country town."

"It will be rather inconvenient, sir. Now, my cousin whom I mentioned to you is quite at home all over the city."

"I am glad to hear it. He will find this knowledge of service—in some other situation," added Mr. Fairchild, significantly.

David Mullins bit his lip and was silent. He could not understand why Felix Gordon, his cousin, had failed to impress Mr. Fairchild favorably. He had not noticed that Felix entered the office with a cigarette in his mouth, which he only threw away when he was introduced to the real estate agent.

"I'll have that boy out of this place within a month, or my name isn't David Mullins," he said to himself.

Chester could not read what was passing through his mind, but he felt instinctively that the bookkeeper was his enemy.

CHAPTER XIII

MR. MULLINS, THE BOOKKEEPER

Chester felt that it was necessary to be on his guard. The bookkeeper was already his enemy. There were two causes for this. First, Mr. Mullins was naturally of an ugly disposition, and, secondly, he was disappointed in not securing the situation for his cousin.

At noon the latter made his appearance. He was a thin, dark-complexioned boy, with curious-looking eyes that somehow inspired distrust.

He walked up to the desk where the book keeper was writing.

"Good-morning, Cousin David," he said.

"Good-morning, Felix. Sit down for a few minutes, and I will take you out to lunch."

"All right!" answered Felix. "Who's that boy?" he inquired, in a low voice.

"The new office boy. Wait till we go out, and I will tell you about it."

In five minutes David Mullins put on his hat and coat and went out with his cousin.

"Stay here and mind the office," he said to Chester, "and if anybody comes in, keep them, if possible. If any tenant comes to pay money, take it and give a receipt."

"All right, sir."

When they were in the street, Felix asked:

"Where did you pick up the boy? Why didn't I get the place?"

"You must ask Mr. Fairchild that. He engaged him without consulting me."

"What sort of a boy is he?"

"A country gawky. He knows nothing of the city."

"Is he a friend of Mr. Fairchild?"

"Fairchild never met him before. Some beggarly artist interceded for him."

"It is too bad I can't be in the office. It would be so nice to be in the same place with you."

"I did my best, but Fairchild didn't seem to fancy you. I think he took a prejudice against you on account of your smoking cigarettes. He must have seen you with one."

"Does the new boy smoke cigarettes?"

"I don't know. That gives me an idea. You had better get

intimate with him and offer him cigarettes. He doesn't know Mr. Fairchild's prejudice, and may fall into the trap."

"How can I get acquainted with him?"

"I'll see to that. I shall be sending him out on an errand presently, and you can offer to go with him."

"That'll do. But you must buy me a package of cigarettes."

"Very well. My plan is to have the boy offend Mr. Fairchild's prejudices, and that may make a vacancy for you. By the way, never let him see you smoking."

"I won't, but as he is not about, I'll smoke a cigarette now."

"Better wait till after lunch."

About ten minutes after Mr. Mullins left the office, a man of forty—evidently a mechanic—entered.

"Is the bookkeeper in?" he asked.

"He's gone to lunch."

"He sent me a bill for this month's rent, which I have already paid."

"Please give me your name."

"James Long."

"And where do you live?"

The address was given—a house on East Twentieth Street.

"Haven't you the receipt?" asked Chester.

"No."

"Didn't Mr. Mullins give you one?"

"Yes; but I carelessly left it on the table. I suppose he found it and kept the money," he added, bitterly.

"But that would be a mean thing to do," said Chester, startled.

"Nothing is too mean for Mullins," said Long. "He's a hard man and a tricky one."

"He will come in soon if you can wait."

"I can't. I am at work, and this is my noon hour."

"I will tell him what you say—"

"Perhaps I may have a chance to call in this afternoon. I feel worried about this matter, for, although it is only ten dollars, that is a good deal to a man with a family, and earning only twelve dollars a week."

Presently Mr. Mullins returned.

"Has anybody been in?" he asked.

"Yes," answered Chester. "A man named James Long."

A curious expression came into the bookkeeper's eye.

"Well, did he pay his rent?"

"No; he said he had paid it already."

"Oh, he did, did he?" sneered the bookkeeper. "In that case, of course he has the receipt."

"No; he said he had left it here on the table, and did not think of it till some time afterwards."

"A likely story. He must think I am a fool. Even a boy like you can see through that."

"He seemed to me like an honest man."

"Oh, well, you are from the country, and could not be expected to know. We have some sharp swindlers in New York."

Chester was quite of that opinion, but he was beginning to think that the description would apply better to David Mullins than to James Long.

"By the way, Chester," said Mr. Mullins, with unusual blandness, "this is my cousin, Felix Gordon."

"Glad to meet you," said Felix, with an artificial smile.

Chester took the extended hand. He was not especially drawn to Felix, but felt that it behooved him to be polite.

"You boys must be somewhere near the same age," said the bookkeeper. "I will give you a chance to become acquainted. Chester, I want you to go to number four seventy-one Bleecker Street. I suppose you don't know where it is?"

"No, sir."

"Felix, go with him and show him the way."

Chester was quite amazed at this unusual and unexpected kindness on the part of a man whom he had regarded as an enemy. Was it possible that he had misjudged him?

The two boys went out together.

When they were fairly in the street, Felix produced his package of cigarettes.

"Have one?" he asked.

"No, thank you; I don't smoke."

"Don't smoke!" repeated Felix, in apparent amusement. "You don't mean that?"

"I never smoked a cigarette in my life."

"Then it's high time you learned. All boys smoke in the city."

"I don't think I should like it."

"Oh, nonsense! Just try one for my sake."

"Thank you, Felix. You are very kind, but I promised mother I wouldn't smoke."

"Your mother lives in the country, doesn't she?"

"Yes."

"Then she won't know it."

"That will make no difference. I made the promise, and I mean to keep it," said Chester, firmly.

"Oh, well, suit yourself. What a muff he is!" thought Felix. "However, he'll soon break over his virtuous resolutions. Do you know," he continued, changing the subject, "that you have got the situation I was after?"

"I think I heard Mr. Mullins say something about it. I am sorry if I have stood in your way."

"Oh, if it hadn't been you it would have been some other boy. How do you think you shall like the city?"

"Very much, I think."

"What pay do you get?"

"Five dollars a week."

"You can't live on that."

"I will try to."

"Of course, it is different with me. I should have lived at home. You'll have to run into debt."

"I will try not to."

"Where do you live?"

"I am staying with a friend—Mr. Conrad, an artist—just now, but I shall soon get a boarding place."

"I live on Eighty-sixth Street—in a flat. My father is in the custom house."

"How long has your cousin—Mr. Mullins—been in this office?"

"About five years. He's awfully smart, cousin David is. It's he that runs the business. Mr. Fairchild is no sort of a business man."

Chester wondered how, under the circumstances, Mr. Mullins should not have influence enough to secure the situation of office boy for Felix.

They soon reached Bleecker Street. Chester took notice of the way in order that he might know it again. He was sharp and observing, and meant to qualify himself for his position as soon as possible.

At five o'clock the office was vacated. Chester remained to sweep up. A piece of paper on the floor attracted his attention. He picked it up and found, to his surprise, that it was James Long's missing receipt. It was on the floor of the clothes closet, and he judged that it had dropped from the bookkeeper's pocket.

What should he do with it?

CHAPTER XIV

THE TABLES TURNED

Under ordinary circumstances, Chester would have handed the receipt to the bookkeeper, but he was convinced that it was the purpose of Mr. Mullins to defraud the tenant out of a month's rent, and he felt that it would not be in the interest of the latter for him to put this power in the hands of the enemy. Obviously the receipt belonged to James Long, who had lost it.

Fortunately, Chester had the address of the mechanic on East Twentieth Street, and he resolved, though it would cost him quite a walk, to call and give him the paper. In twenty minutes after locking the office he found himself in front of a large tenement house, which was occupied by a great number of families. He found that Long lived on the third floor back.

He knocked at the door. It was opened to him by a woman of forty, who had a babe in her arms, while another—a little girl —was holding onto her dress.

"Does Mr. James Long live here?" asked Chester.

"Yes."

"Is he at home?"

"No, but I am expecting him home from work every minute. Will you come in, or shall I give him your message?"

"Perhaps I had better see him, if it won't inconvenience you."

"Oh, no, if you will excuse my poor rooms," said Mrs. Long, pleasantly.

"I am poor myself, and am not used to fine rooms."

"Take the rocking-chair," said Mrs. Long, offering him the best chair in the room. "If you will excuse me, I will go on preparing my husband's supper."

"Certainly. Shall I take the baby?"

"Oh, I wouldn't like to trouble you."

"I like babies."

Chester had seen that the baby's face was clean, and that it looked attractive. Babies know their friends instinctively, and this particular baby was soon in a frolic with its young guardian.

"I guess you are used to babies," said the mother, pleased.

"No, I am the only baby in my family, but I am fond of children."

I may remark here that manly boys generally do like children, and I haven't much respect for those who will tease or tyrannize over them.

In ten minutes a heavy step was heard on the stairs, and James Long entered. His face was sober, for, after his interview with Chester Rand—he had not had time for a second call—he began to fear that he should have to pay his month's rent over again, and this to him would involve a severe loss.

He looked with surprise at Chester, not immediately recognizing him.

"I come from Mr. Fairchild's office," explained Chester.

"Oh, yes; I remember seeing you there. Has the receipt been found?" he added, eagerly.

"Yes."

James Long looked very much relieved.

"I am very glad," he sighed. "Mr. Mullins wouldn't have believed me. What does he say now?"

"He doesn't know that the receipt is found."

"How is that?" asked the mechanic, puzzled.

"I found it after Mr. Mullins went away."

"Where did you find it?"

"In the clothes closet, just under where Mr. Mullins hangs his coat," added Chester, significantly.

"And you bring it to me?"

"Yes, it belongs to you. Besides, after what I heard, I didn't dare to trust it in the hands of the bookkeeper."

"I see you think the same of him as I do."

"I don't like him."

"You think he meant to cheat me?"

"It looks like it."

"I am all right now. What do you think I had better do?"

"Come round to-morrow, but don't show the receipt unless Mr. Fairchild is in the office. He is a very different man from Mr. Mullins. The bookkeeper might still play a trick upon you?"

"I believe you're right. Shall I tell him how you found and gave me back the receipt?"

"No; let Mr. Mullins puzzle over it. It is fortunate he didn't destroy the receipt, or you would have had no resource."

"You're a smart boy, and I'll take your advice. How long have you been in the office?"

"This is my first day," answered Chester, smiling.

"Well, well! I couldn't have believed it. You will make a smart business man. You've been a good friend to James Long, and he won't forget it. I say, wife, perhaps this young gentleman will stay to supper."

"Thank you," answered Chester. "I would, but I am to meet a friend uptown at six o'clock. It is so late," he added, looking at the clock on the mantel, "that I must go at once."

When Chester met his friend the artist, he told him of what

had happened.

"That Mullins is evidently a rascal, and a very mean one," said Mr. Conrad. "If I were going to defraud anyone, it wouldn't be a poor mechanic."

"Mr. Mullins has already taken a dislike to me. If he should discover that I have found the receipt and given it to Mr. Long, he would hate me even worse."

"You must look out for him. He will bear watching."

"I wish he were more like Mr. Fairchild. He seems a fair, honorable man."

"He is. I don't understand why he should employ such a fellow as Mullins."

"Perhaps he hasn't found him out."

"Mullins will find it hard to explain this matter. Let me know how it comes out. I suppose Long will call at the office to-morrow?"

"Yes; I advised him to."

The next day, about twenty minutes after twelve, James Long entered the office. He looked about him anxiously, and, to his relief, saw that Mr. Fairchild was present. He went up to the table where the broker was seated.

"I came about my rent," he said.

"You can speak to Mr. Mullins," said the broker, going on with his writing.

"I would rather speak with you, sir."

"How is that?" asked Mr. Fairchild, his attention excited.

"I will tell you, sir," said the bookkeeper, with an ugly look. "This man came here yesterday and declined to pay his rent, because, he said, he had paid it already."

"And I had," said Long, quietly. "I am a mechanic on small wages, and I can't afford to pay my rent twice."

"Did you pay the rent to Mr. Mullins?"

"Yes, sir."

"When?"

"Day before yesterday."

"Then he gave you a receipt?"

"He did, sir."

"It seems to me that than settles the question. Did you give him a receipt, Mr. Mullins?"

"If I had, he could show it now. He says that he left it behind in the office here. Of course, that's too thin!"

"It is very important to take good care of your receipt, Mr. Long."

"Did you ever lose or mislay a receipt, sir?"

"Yes, I have on two or three occasions."

"So that I am not the only one to whom it has happened."

"Mr. Mullins, did Mr. Long come to the office on the day when he says he paid the rent?"

"Yes, sir."

"And he didn't pay it?"

"No, sir. He said he hadn't the money, but would bring it in a few days."

James Long listened in indignant astonishment.

"That is untrue, sir. I made no excuse, but handed Mr. Mullins the amount in full."

"There is a very extraordinary discrepancy in your statements. You say that he wrote out a receipt?"

"Yes, sir."

"It is a pity that you can't produce it."

"Yes," chimed in Mullins, with a sneer, "it is unlucky that you cannot produce it."

Then came a sensation.

"I can produce it," said Long. "The receipt has been found," and he drew out the slip of paper and passed it to Mr. Fairchild.

The face of Mullins was a study. His amazement was deep and genuine.

"It must be a forgery," he said. "Mr. Long can't possibly have a receipt."

"You are mistaken," said Mr. Fairchild. "The receipt and the signature are genuine, and it is written on one of our letter heads."

Mullins took the receipt and faltered:

"I don't understand it."

"Nor do I," said the broker, sternly. "Did you make any entry on the books?"

"I—I don't remember."

"Show me the record."

Mr. Fairchild opened the book, and saw an entry made, but afterward erased.

When the bookkeeper found the receipt on the table, a promising piece of rascality was suggested to him. He would keep the money himself, and conceal the record.

"Mr. Long," said the broker, "here is your receipt. It is clear that you have paid your rent. You will have no more trouble."

Then, as the mechanic left the office, the broker, turning to the bookkeeper, said, sternly:

"Another such transaction, Mr. Mullins, and you leave my employ."

"But, sir—" stammered Mullins.

"You may spare your words. I understand the matter. If you had not been in my employ so long, I would discharge you at the end of this week."

Mullins went back to his desk, crushed and mortified. But his brain was busy with the thought, "Where could James Long have obtained the receipt?" He remembered having put it into the pocket of his overcoat, and it had disappeared.

"I was a fool that I didn't destroy it," he reflected.

CHAPTER XV

A PLOT AGAINST CHESTER

The more the bookkeeper thought of it, the more he was of the opinion that Chester must have had something to do with the events that led to his discovery and humiliation. Otherwise, how could James Long have recovered the receipt? He, himself, had found it and kept it in his possession. Chester must have chanced upon the receipt and carried it to Long.

Though well convinced of it, he wished to find out positively. Accordingly, he took his cousin Felix into his confidence as far as was necessary, and sent him to the room of the mechanic to find out whether Chester had been there.

It was the middle of the forenoon when Felix knocked at the door of James Long's humble home.

Mrs. Long, with the baby in her arms, answered the knock.

"Is this Mrs. Long?" asked Felix.

"Yes, sir."

"I am the friend of Chester Rand."

"I don't think I know Mr. Rand," said Mrs. Long, who had not heard Chester's name.

"The boy from Mr. Fairchild's office. He called here, I believe, one day last week."

"Oh, yes and a good friend he was to me and mine."

"In what way?" asked Felix, his face lighting with satisfaction at the discovery he had made.

"He brought my husband the receipt he had lost. Didn't he tell you?"

"Oh, yes. I wasn't thinking of that. He asked me to inquire if he left his gloves here?"

"I haven't found any. I should have seen them if he left them here."

"All right. I will tell him. He thought he might have left them. Good morning, ma'am."

And Felix hurried downstairs. He was not partial to poor people or tenement houses, and he was glad to get away.

He reached the office in time to go out to lunch with the bookkeeper.

"Well?" asked Mullins, eagerly. "Did you go to Long's?"

"Yes."

"What did you find out?"

"I found out that your office boy had been there and carried them the receipt."

"The young—viper! So he is trying to undermine me in the office. Well, he'll live to regret it," and the bookkeeper shook his head vigorously.

"I'd get even with him if I were you, Cousin David."

"Trust me for that! I generally pay off all debts of that kind."

"How will you do it?" asked Felix, curiously.

"I don't know yet. Probably I'll get him into some bad scrape that will secure his discharge."

"And then you'll get me into the place?"

"I am afraid I can't. I am not on good terms with Mr. Fairchild, and my recommendation won't do you much good, even if I do manage to get rid of Chester."

"Then I don't see how I am going to be benefited by working for you," said Felix, dissatisfied.

"I'll pay you in some way. To begin with, here's a dollar. This is for your errand of this morning."

"Thank you, Cousin David," said Felix, pocketing the bill with an air of satisfaction. "I think I'll go to Daly's Theater to-night. Father doesn't give me much spending money— only twenty-five cents a week, and what's a fellow to do with such a beggarly sum as that?"

"It is more than I had at your age."

"The world has progressed since then. A boy needs more

pocket money now than he did fifteen years ago. How soon shall you try to get even with that boy?"

"I think it will be prudent to wait a while. Mr. Fairchild may suspect something if I move too soon. The boy has been with us less than a week."

"He has been with you long enough to do some harm."

"That's true," said Mullins, with an ugly look.

"Does he seem to suit Mr. Fairchild?"

"Yes; he appears to be intelligent, and he attends to his duties—worse luck!—but he's a thorn in my side, a thorn in my side! I'd give twenty-five dollars if he was out of the office."

"Do you want me to break off acquaintance with him?"

"No; keep on good terms with him. Let him think you are his intimate friend. It will give me a chance to plot against him—through you."

Horatio Alger, Jr

CHAPTER XVI

PROF. HAZLITT AT HOME

Chester did not forget his engagement to call upon Prof. Hazlitt on Wednesday evening.

He was shown at once into the professor's study. It was a large room, the sides lined with bookcases crowded with volumes. There seemed to be more books than Chester had ever seen before.

In the center of the room was a study table, covered with books, open as if in use. On one side was a desk, at which Prof. Hazlitt himself was seated.

"Good-evening, my young friend," he said, cordially, as Chester entered the room. "You did not forget your appointment."

"No, sir. I was not likely to forget such an engagement."

"Have you grown to feel at home in the city?"

"Not entirely, sir, but I am getting a little used to it."

"I think you mentioned that you were going into a real

estate office?"

"Yes, sir. I have commenced my duties there."

"I hope you find them agreeable."

"I might, sir, but that the bookkeeper seems to have taken a dislike to me."

"I suspect that you would like better to devote yourself to art work."

"I think I should, sir, but Mr. Conrad thinks it better that I should only devote my leisure to drawing."

"No doubt his advice is wise, for the present, at least. Now, suppose we come to business. I believe I told you I am writing a book on ethnology."

"Yes, sir."

"I find a good deal of help in rare volumes which I consult at the Astor Library. These I cannot borrow, but I have the use of anything I find suited to my needs in the library of Columbia College. Then I import a good many books. I shall spare no pains to make my own work valuable and comprehensive. Of course, I shall feel at liberty to copy and use any illustrations I find in foreign publications. It is here that you can help me."

"Yes, sir."

"Here, for instance," and the professor opened a French book, "are some sketches illustrating the dress and appearance of the natives of Madagascar. Do you think you can copy them?"

"I have no doubt of it, sir," he answered.

"Sit down in that chair and try. You will find pencils and drawing paper before you. I will mention one or two particulars in which I want you to deviate from the original."

Chester sat down and was soon deep in his task. He felt that it was important for him to do his best. He could understand that, though the professor was a kind-hearted man, he would be a strict critic.

He therefore worked slowly and carefully, and it was nearly an hour before he raised his head and said:

"I have finished."

"Show the sketch to me," said the professor.

Chester handed it to him.

He examined it with critical attention. Gradually his face lighted up with pleasure.

"Admirably done!" he exclaimed. "You have carried out my wishes."

"Then you are satisfied, sir?"

"Entirely."

"I am very glad," said Chester, with an air of relief.

He felt now he could do all that was required of him, and, as the contract would pay him two hundred dollars, this success to-night was an important one.

"I won't ask you to do any more this evening, but I will give you some work to do at home. I believe I agreed to pay you two dollars for each sketch?"

"Yes, sir."

"Probably you are not over well provided with money, and I will pay you as you go on. Or, rather, I will give you ten dollars as an advance for future work."

"Thank you, sir. You are very kind."

"Only considerate. I have seen the time when a ten-dollar-bill would have been welcome to me. Now, thanks to a wealthy relative, who left me a fortune, I am amply provided for."

At this moment the study door opened and a bright-looking boy of about fifteen entered.

"May I come in, uncle?" he asked, with a smile.

"Yes. Chester, this is my nephew, Arthur Burks. Arthur, this is Chester Rand, a young artist, who is assisting me."

Arthur came forward and gave Chester his hand cordially.

"You ought to wear spectacles," he said, "like uncle Edgar. You don't look dignified enough to be his assistant."

"That may come in time," said Chester, with a smile.

"Arthur, I am done with Chester for this evening," said the professor. "You may carry him off and entertain him. You may bring me the other two sketches whenever you are ready."

"Come up to my den," said Arthur. "I have the front room on the third floor."

As they went upstairs, a prolonged, melancholy shriek rang through the house.

Chester stopped short in dismay, and an expression of pain succeeded the gay look on Arthur's face.

CHAPTER XVII

CHESTER TAKES A LESSON IN BOXING

"That is my poor, little cousin," explained Arthur.

"Is he sick or in pain?" asked Chester, in quick sympathy.

"He had a fever when he was three years old that left his mind a wreck. He is now eight. The most eminent physicians have seen him, but there seems little hope of his improvement or recovery."

"Does he suffer pain?"

"You ask on account of the shriek you heard. As far as we can tell, he does not. The shriek comes, so the doctor tells us, from a nervous spasm. He would have been a bright boy if he had kept his health. Would you like to see him?"

Chester shrank back.

"I am afraid I should excite him," he said.

He had, besides, an idea that a boy so afflicted would be repulsive in appearance.

"No," said Arthur, "it may relieve him to see you by diverting his thoughts."

Without further words, he opened the door of a room at the head of the staircase and entered, followed reluctantly by Chester.

"Ernest," said Arthur, in a soothing tone, "I have brought you a friend. His name is Chester."

Chester was amazed at the sight of the boy. He was wonderfully handsome, especially when at Arthur's words the look of pain left his face and it brightened into radiant beauty. He seemed to fall in love with Chester at first sight. He ran up to him, seized his hand, kissed it, and said:

"I love you."

Arthur, too, looked amazed.

"He never took to anyone so before," he said. "You have fascinated him."

"Sit down. Let me sit in your lap," pleaded Ernest.

All feeling of repugnance, all thoughts of the boy's malady were forgotten. Chester sat in a low rocking-chair and Ernest seated himself in his lap, touching his face and hair softly with a caressing hand.

"What a charming boy he is!" thought Chester.

"Did you come to see me?" asked Ernest, softly.

"Yes, I came with Arthur."

"Will you stay with me a little while?"

"A little while, but I must soon go. Why did you scream so loud a little while ago?"

"I—don't know."

"Were you in pain?"

"N—no," answered Ernest, softly.

"Do you like to cry out in that manner?"

"No, but—I have to do it. I can't help it."

"I think he gives the right explanation," said Arthur. "It is a nervous impulse, and has nothing to do with pain."

"Does he ever sit in your lap, like this?"

"No; I think he likes me in a way, for I am always kind to him, but you seem to draw him to you irresistibly."

At that moment the professor came in. When he saw Ernest sitting in Chester's lap, he stopped short in astonishment.

"This is strange," he said.

"Isn't it, uncle? Chester seems to fascinate my little cousin. No sooner did he enter the room than Ernest ran up to him, kissed his hand, and caressed him."

"I can't explain it," said the professor, "but Chester seems to have a wonderful influence over my poor boy. I never saw him look so happy or contented before."

All this while Ernest continued to stroke Chester's cheek and his hair, and regarded him with looks of fond affection.

"I am afraid Ernest annoys you," said the professor.

"No; I am glad he likes me. I never had a little brother. I think I should enjoy having one."

"If he could only be always like this," said the professor, regretfully.

Just then Margaret entered. She was the nurse, who had constant charge of Ernest. She paused on the threshold, and her looks showed her surprise.

"Ernest has found a friend, Margaret," said the professor.

"I never saw the like, sir. Come here, Ernest."

The boy shook his head.

"No, I want to stay with him," indicating Chester.

"Did Ernest ever see him before, sir?"

"No; it seems to be a case of love at first sight."

"He has cut me out," said Arthur, smiling. "Ernest, which do you like best, me or him?"

"Him," answered Ernest, touching Chester's cheek.

"I must tell Dr. Gridley of this new manifestation on the part of my poor boy," said the professor. "Perhaps he can interpret it."

For twenty minutes Chester retained Ernest on his lap. Then Arthur said:

"Chester must go now, Ernest."

The boy left Chester's lap obediently.

"Will you come and see me again?" he pleaded.

"Yes, I will come," said Chester, and, stooping over, he kissed the boy's cheek. Ernest's face lighted up with a loving smile, and again he kissed Chester's hand.

"Now, Chester, you can come to my den." Arthur opened the door of a large room, furnished with every comfort.

It was easy to see that it was a boy's apartment. On a table were boxing gloves. Over a desk in a corner was hung the photograph of a football team, of which Arthur was the captain. There was another photograph representing him with gloves on, about to have a set-to with a boy friend.

"Do you box, Chester?" he asked.

"No; I never saw a pair of boxing gloves before."

"I will give you a lesson. Here, put on this pair."

Chester smiled.

"I shall be at your mercy," he said. "I am, perhaps, as strong as you, but I have no science."

"It won't take you long to learn."

So the two boys faced each other. Before he knew what was

going to happen, Chester received a light tap on the nose from his new friend.

"I must tell you how to guard yourself. I will be the professor and you the pupil."

Chester soon became interested, and at the end of half an hour his teacher declared that he had improved wonderfully.

"We will have a lesson every time you come to see uncle," he said.

"Then I shall come to see two professors."

"Yes, an old one and young one. Between uncle, Ernest and myself, you will find your time pretty well occupied when you come here."

"I think it a great privilege to come here," said Chester, gratefully.

"And I am glad to have you. I shall have some one to box with, at any rate. Now," he added, with a comical look, "I can't induce my uncle to have a bout with me. Indeed, I should be afraid to, for he is so shortsighted he would need to wear spectacles, and I would inevitably break them."

Chester could not forbear laughing at the idea of the learned professor having a boxing match with his lively, young nephew.

"If you will make me as good a boxer as yourself, I shall feel very much indebted."

"That will come in time. I am quite flattered at the opportunity of posing as a teacher. Have you a taste for jewelry? Just look in this drawer."

Arthur opened one of the small drawers in his bureau, and displayed a varied collection of studs, sleeve buttons, collar buttons, scarf pins, etc.

"You might set up a jeweler's store," suggested Chester. "Where did you get them all?"

"I had an uncle who was in the business, and he and other relatives have given me plenty."

"I haven't even a watch."

"No, really? Why, how can you get along without one?"

"I have to."

"Wait a minute."

Arthur opened another drawer, revealing two silver watches, one an open face, the other a hunting watch.

"Take your choice," he said.

"Do you really mean it?"

"Certainly."

"But would your uncle approve of your giving me such a valuable present?"

"My uncle doesn't bother himself about such trifles. I don't use either of these watches. I have a gold one, given me last Christmas."

"Since you are so kind, I think I prefer the hunting watch."

"All right! There it is. Let me set it for you. The chain goes with it, of course."

Chester felt delighted with his present. He had hoped some-time—when he was eighteen, perhaps—to own a watch, but had no expectation of getting one so soon.

"You are a generous friend, Arthur," he said.

"Don't make too much of such a trifle, Chester!" returned the other, lightly.

When Chester said he must go home, Arthur put on his hat and proposed to walk with him part of the way, an offer which Chester gratefully accepted.

They walked over to Broadway, chatting as they went.

All at once, Chester, who had not expected to see anyone he knew, touched Arthur on the arm.

"Do you see that man in front of us?" he asked, pointing to a figure about six feet ahead.

"Yes. What of him?"

"It is our bookkeeper, David Mullins."

"Is it, indeed? Do you know whom he is walking with?"

Chester glanced at a rather flashily dressed individual who was walking arm in arm with the bookkeeper.

"No," he answered.

"It is Dick Ralston," answered Arthur, "one of the most notorious gamblers in the city."

Horatio Alger, Jr

CHAPTER XVIII

DICK RALSTON

Chester was new to the city and a novice in worldly affairs, but the discovery that the bookkeeper was on intimate terms with a gambler astounded him. He felt that Mr. Fairchild ought to know it, but he shrank from telling him.

Of course, the presumption was that Mullins was also a gambler, but this was not certain. Chester decided to say nothing, but to be watchful. David Mullins had been five years in his present place, and his services must have been satisfactory or he would not have been retained.

There was one thing, however, that Chester did not know. This gambler—Dick Ralston, as he was familiarly called—was only a recent acquaintance. Mullins had known him but three months, but had already, through his influence, been smitten by the desire to become rich more quickly than he could in any legitimate way.

He had accompanied Dick to the gaming table, and tried his luck, losing more than he could comfortably spare. He was in debt to his dangerous friend one hundred and fifty dollars, and on the evening in question Dick had intimated that he was in need of the money.

"But how can I give it to you?" asked Mullins, in a tone of annoyance.

"You receive a good salary."

"One hundred dollars a month, yes. But I can't spare more than thirty dollars a month toward paying the debt."

"Which would take you five months. That won't suit me. Haven't you got any money saved up?"

"No; I ought to have, but I have enjoyed myself as I went along, and it has taken all I earned."

"Humph! Very pleasant for me!"

"And for me, too. It isn't very satisfactory to pinch and scrape for five months just to get out of debt. If it was for articles I had had—in other words, for value received—it would be different. But it is just for money lost at the gaming table—a gambling debt."

"Such debts, among men of honor," said Dick, loftily, "are the most binding. Everywhere they are debts of honor."

"I don't see why," grumbled Mullins.

"Come," said Ralston, soothingly, "you are out of sorts, and can't see things in their right light. I'll lend you fifty dollars more, making the debt two hundred dollars."

"I don't see how that will help me."

"I'll tell you. You must win the money to pay your debt at the gaming table. Why, two hundred dollars is a trifle. You might win it in one evening."

"Or lose as much more."

"There's no such word as fail! Shall I tell you what I did once?"

"Yes," answered Mullins, in some curiosity.

"I was in Nashville—dead broke! I was younger then, and losses affected me more. I was even half inclined—you will laugh, I know—to blow my brains out or to throw myself into the river, when a stranger offered to lend me ten dollars to try my luck again. Well, I thought as you did, that it was of little use. I would lose it, and so make matters worse.

"But desperation led me to accept. It was one chance, not a very good one, but still a chance. From motives of prudence I only risked five dollars at first. I lost. Savagely I threw down the remaining five and won twenty-five. Then I got excited, and kept on for an hour. At the end of that time, how do you think I stood?"

"How?" asked Mullins, eagerly.

"I had won eight hundred and sixty-five dollars," answered Dick Ralston, coolly. "I paid back the ten dollars, and went out of the gambling house a rich man, comparatively speaking."

Now, all this story was a clever fiction, but David Mullins did not know this. He accepted it as plain matter of fact, and his heart beat quickly as he fancied himself winning as large a sum.

"But such cases must be rare," he ventured.

"Not at all. I could tell you more wonderful stories about

friends of mine, though it was the luckiest thing that ever happened to me. Now, will you take the fifty dollars I offered you?"

"Yes, but I don't want to play again to-night. I feel nervous."

"Very good. Meet me to-morrow evening at the gambling house, and the money shall be ready for you."

Then they parted, and the bookkeeper, who had a headache, went home and to bed. He had that evening lost fifty dollars to Dick Ralston, and so increased his debt from one hundred to one hundred and fifty dollars.

But his heart was filled with feverish excitement. The story told by Ralston had its effect upon him, and he decided to keep on in the dangerous path upon which he had entered. Why pinch himself for five months to pay his debt, when a single evening's luck would clear him from every obligation? If Dick Ralston and others could be lucky, why not he? This was the way Mullins reasoned. He never stopped to consider what would be the result if things did not turn out as he hoped—if he lost instead of won.

Some weeks passed. The bookkeeper met with varying success at the gaming table. Sometimes he won, sometimes he lost, but on the whole his debt to Dick Ralston didn't increase. There were reasons why the gambler decided to go slow. He was playing with Mullins as a cat plays with a mouse.

But our chief concern is with Chester Rand. He found a comfortable room on Twelfth Street, not far from the office, which, with board, only cost him five dollars per week. This, to be sure, took all his salary, but he was earning something outside.

On account of so much time being taken up by his work for the professor, he did little for the comic weeklies. But occasionally, through his friend, the artist, a five or ten-dollar bill came into his hands. He bought himself a new suit, and some other articles which he found he needed, and wrote home to ask his mother if she wished any assistance.

"Thank you for your offer," she replied, "but the money Miss Dolby pays me defrays all my housekeeping expenses and a little more. She is certainly peculiar, but is good-natured, and never finds fault. She is a good deal of company for me. Of course, I miss you very much, but it cheers me to think you are doing well, and are happy, with good prospects for the future. There is nothing for you in Wyncombe, as I very well know; that is, nothing you would be willing to accept.

"That reminds me to say that Mr. Tripp is having a hard time with boys. He discharged Abel Wood soon after you went to New York. He has tried two boys since, but doesn't seem to get suited. When I was in the store yesterday, he inquired after you. 'Tell him,' he said, 'that if he gets tired of New York, he can come back to the store, and I will pay him three dollars a week!" He said this with an air of a man who is making a magnificent offer. I told him you were satisfied with your position in the city. I must tell you of one mean thing he has done.

"He has been trying to induce Miss Dolby to leave me and take board with him, offering to take her for two dollars a week less. She told me of this herself. 'I wouldn't go there if he'd take me for nothing,' she said, and I believe she meant it. She is not mean, and is willing to pay a fair, even a liberal, price, where she is suited. You see, therefore, that neither you nor I need borrow any trouble on this point!"

This letter relieved Chester of all anxiety. All things seemed bright to him. What he did for the comic weeklies, added to his work for Prof. Hazlitt, brought him in ten dollars a week on an average. This, added to the five dollars a week from Mr. Fairchild, gave him an aggregate salary of fifteen dollars a week, so that he was always amply provided with money.

"Cousin David," said Felix to the bookkeeper one day, "I don't see how it happens that Chester is so well supplied with cash."

"Is he?" asked Mullins.

"Yes; he has just bought a new suit, a new hat and new shoes. They must have cost him altogether as much as thirty dollars. How much wages do you pay him?"

"Five dollars a week."

"And he pays all that for board, for he told me so."

"It does seem a little mysterious. Perhaps his friend the artist helps him."

"No, he doesn't. I intimated as much one day, but he said no, that he paid his own way. One evening last week, I saw him going into Daly's Theatre with a young fellow handsomely dressed—quite a young swell. They had two-dollar seats, and I learned that Chester paid for them. He doesn't have any chance to pick up any money in this office, does he?" asked Felix, significantly.

"I can't say as to that. I haven't missed any."

"I wish he would help himself. Of course, he would be discharged, and then you might find a place for me."

"I may do so yet."

"Is there any chance of it?" asked Felix, eagerly.

"In about two weeks, Mr. Fairchild is going West on business. He will be gone for a month, probably. In his absence, I shall run the office."

"I see."

"And I shall probably find some reason for discharging Chester Rand," added the bookkeeper, significantly. "In that case, you will hold yourself ready to slip into his place."

"Bully for you, Cousin David," exclaimed Felix, in exultation.

CHAPTER XIX

MR. FAIRCHILD LEAVES THE CITY

About ten days later, Chester found himself alone in the office with his employer, the bookkeeper having gone out to call upon a man who had commissioned the broker to buy him a house.

"Chester," said Mr. Fairchild, "has Mr. Mullins mentioned to you that I start next Monday on a Western trip?"

"I heard him say so to a gentleman in here on business."

"I shall have to leave Mr. Mullins to take charge of the office and run the business. The time was when I would have done so with confidence, but the affair of James Long has made me distrustful. He thoroughly understands my business, and it would be difficult for me to supply his place. For the present, therefore, I feel obliged to retain him. During my absence, however, I wish, if you see anything wrong, that you would apprise me of it by letter. You may direct letters to Palmer's Hotel, Chicago, and they will be forwarded to me from there. What is your address?"

Chester gave it, and Mr. Fairchild wrote it down.

"It is rather unusual," continued Mr. Fairchild, "for a man in my position to make a confidant of his office boy, but I have observed you carefully, and I believe that you are not only intelligent, but are faithful to my interests."

"Thank you, sir," said Chester, with genuine gratification. "I think I can promise you that you will not be disappointed in me."

"Of course Mr. Mullins must not know of the understanding between us. Don't breathe a hint of what I have said."

"No, sir, I will not."

"In case you think it necessary you may telegraph to me. I hope, however, that no such emergency will arise."

Chester asked himself whether it was his duty to apprise Mr. Fairchild of his seeing Mullins in intimate companionship with a gambler, but, on the whole, decided not to do so. He did not wish needlessly to prejudice his employer against the bookkeeper.

On Monday morning Mr. Fairchild left the office and took the Sixth Avenue Elevated train to Cortlandt Street station, from which it is only five minutes' walk to the ferry connecting with the train on the Pennsylvania Railroad.

"How long shall you be away, Mr. Fairchild?" asked the bookkeeper.

"I cannot yet tell. It will depend on the success I meet with in my business. I am afraid I may be absent four weeks."

"Don't hurry back," said Mullins. "I will keep things running."

"I rely upon your fidelity," said the broker, not without significance.

"You may be assured of that. I have been in your employ for over five years."

"And of course understand all the details of my business. That is true. Continue faithful to me and you will have no cause to repent it."

"Thank you, sir. You need have no anxiety."

"Chester," said Mr. Fairchild, "you may go with me as far as the station and carry my grip."

When they were outside, the broker said:

"I could have carried the grip myself, but I wished to have a parting word with you. Mr. Mullins is thoroughly acquainted with my business, but within the last six months I found myself distrusting him. In four weeks, for I shall be likely to be away that length of time, something may occur detrimental to my interests, and I heartily wish I had some one else in charge. I may rely upon you bearing in mind what I told you the other day?"

"Yes, sir; I won't forget."

"I know that you are faithful, and I only wish you understood the business well enough to be placed in charge."

"I wish so, too," said Chester, frankly.

"I think, however," Mr. Fairchild added, with a smile, "that it would be hardly prudent to trust my business to an office boy."

"You are already trusting me very much, Mr. Fairchild."

"Yes; I feel safe in doing so."

Chester took the grip up the Elevated stairway and parted with Mr. Fairchild at the ticket office.

As he went down to the street he reflected that his own position during the broker's absence might not be very comfortable. Still he had his employer's confidence, and that gave him much pleasure.

He had reached Harris' large store on his way home when a rakish-looking figure, springing from he knew not where, overtook and touched him on the arm. Chester immediately recognized him as the gambler with whom he had seen the bookkeeper walking on the evening of his first visit to the house of Prof. Hazlitt.

"I say, boy," said Ralston, "you're employed by Fairchild, the real estate man, ain't you?"

"Yes, sir," answered Chester, coldly.

"Didn't I see him going to the Elevated station with you just now?"

"Yes, sir."

"With a grip in his hand?"

"Yes."

"Is he off for a journey?"

"He has started for the West."

"So? I had business with him, but I suppose I can transact it with Mullins just as well."

"You will find him in the office."

"All right! I'll go there."

Chester turned his glance upon Dick Ralston and rapidly took note of his appearance. He was rather a stocky man, with a red, pimpled face, a broad nose, small, twinkling eyes and intensely black hair. He wore a "loud," striped sack suit, and on one of his pudgy fingers was a diamond ring. It was really a diamond, and he had often found it serviceable. When he was in very bad luck he pawned it for a comfortable sum, but invariably redeemed it when fortune smiled upon him again.

He followed Chester into the broker's office. Mullins sat on a stool at the desk, picking his teeth. He looked like a man of leisure, with little upon his mind.

"Hello, Mullins, old boy!" said Dick, pushing forward with extended hand. "So you're promoted to boss?"

"Yes," answered the bookkeeper, showing his teeth in a complacent smile. "Can I sell you a house this morning?"

"Well, not exactly. I'm not quite up to that in the present state of my funds. If you have on your list a one-story shanty on the rocks near Central Park I may invest."

"Cash down, or do you want to have part of the purchase money on mortgage?"

Then both laughed, and Ralston made a playful dig at Mullins' ribs.

Chester could not help hearing the conversation. He saw in it a proof of the friendly relations between the two. This, so far as he knew, was the first visit made by Ralston to Mr. Mullins. It was clear that the bookkeeper felt that such a caller would injure him in the eyes of Mr. Fairchild.

"I am glad old Fairchild is gone," said Dick Ralston, lowering his tone. "Now I can come in freely."

"Don't come in too often," replied Mullins, with a cautioning look at Chester. "It might—"

Chester lost the rest of the sentence.

"Send him out!" suggested Dick, in a still lower tone, but Chester caught the words.

"Chester," said the bookkeeper, "you may go up to the Fifth Avenue Hotel and ask at the office if Mr. Paul Perkins, of Minneapolis, has arrived?"

"Yes, sir."

After Chester went out, Ralston inquired, "Is there a man named Paul Perkins?"

"Not that I know of," answered Mullins, with a laugh.

"I see. You're a sharp fellow. You only wanted to get rid of the kid."

"Exactly. Now we can talk freely."

"That's what I came about. Do you know, Mullins, you are owing me seven hundred and fifty dollars?"

"Is it so much as that?" asked the bookkeeper, anxiously.

"Yes; I can show you the account. Now, to tell you the truth, Mullins, I'm in a tight fix, and my bank account needs replenishing."

"So does mine," returned Mullins, with a sickly smile.

Dick Ralston frowned slightly.

"No joking, please!" he said, roughly. "I'm in earnest."

"I don't see what I am going to do about it," muttered Mullins, defiantly.

"Don't you. Then perhaps I can help you by a suggestion."

"I wish you would."

"You are left in charge here during Mr. Fairchild's absence?"

"Well, suppose I am."

"And you handle the funds?"

"Yes."

"Then," and Dick Ralston bent over and whispered something in the bookkeeper's ear.

Mullins started, and looked agitated.

"What would you have me do?" he inquired.

"Borrow a little money from the office," answered Dick, coolly.

"But, good heavens, man, it would ruin me. Must you have me risk prison?"

"Don't be alarmed! I only want you to borrow two or three hundred dollars. You can return it before Fairchild gets back."

"How am I to return it?"

"You can win it back in one evening at the gaming table."

"Or lose more."

There was considerable further conversation, Dick Ralston urging, and Mullins feebly opposing something which the gambler proposed. Then a customer came in, who had to receive attention. Inside of an hour Chester re-entered the office, accompanied by a sandy-complexioned stranger, his head covered with a broad, flapping, Western sombrero, and wearing a long, brown beard descending at least eighteen inches.

"I hear you want to see me," he said to Mullins.

"Who are you?" asked the astonished bookkeeper.

"I am Paul Perkins, of Minneapolis," was the surprising reply.

CHAPTER XX

PAUL PERKINS, OF MINNEAPOLIS

If a bomb had exploded in the office David Mullins and his friend Ralston could not have been more astonished than by the appearance of Paul Perkins, whose name was invented without the slightest idea that any such person existed.

Before relating what followed, a word of explanation is necessary.

Chester went to the Fifth Avenue Hotel without the slightest suspicion that he had been sent on a fool's errand. He imagined, indeed, that Mr. Mullins wanted to get rid of him, but did not doubt that there was such a man as Paul Perkins, and that he was expected to arrive at the Fifth Avenue Hotel.

He walked up Broadway in a leisurely manner, feeling that his hasty return was not desired. He reached the Fifth Avenue, and entering—it was the first time he had ever visited the hotel—went up to the desk.

The clerk was giving instructions to a bell boy, who was directed to carry a visitor's card to No. 221. When at leisure, Chester asked:

"Has Mr. Paul Perkins, of Minneapolis, arrived at the hotel?"

The clerk looked over the list of arrivals. Finally his forefinger stopped at an entry on the book.

"Yes," he answered, "he arrived last evening. Did you wish to see him?"

About this Chester was in doubt. He had only been asked to inquire if Mr. Perkins had arrived. He assumed, however, that the bookkeeper wished to see Mr. Perkins at the office. Accordingly he answered, "Yes, sir. I should like to see him."

The clerk rang a bell and another bell boy made his appearance.

"Write your name on a card," said the clerk, "and I will send it up."

"The gentleman won't know my name," said Chester.

"Then give the name of your firm."

So Chester, after slight hesitation, wrote:

"Chester Rand. From Clement Fairchild, Real Estate Broker."

"Take that up to 169," said the clerk to the bell boy.

In five minutes the boy returned.

"Mr. Perkins says you are to come upstairs to his room," he reported.

Chester followed the bell boy to the elevator.

He had never before ridden in such a conveyance and the sensation was a novel one. They got off at one of the upper floors, and Chester followed his guide to the door of a room near by.

The bell boy knocked.

"Come in," was heard from the inside.

Chester entered and found himself in the presence of a man of fifty, with a sandy complexion and thick, brown beard. He held the card in his hand, and was looking at it.

"Are you Chester Rand?" he asked, in a high-pitched voice.

"Yes, sir."

"And you come from Clement Fairchild?"

"Yes, sir."

"This is very curious. I never heard the name before."

Chester looked surprised.

"I can't explain it, sir," he said. "I was asked to come to the hotel and ask if you had arrived."

"Where is Mr. Fairchild's office?"

"On West Fourteenth Street."

"And he is a real estate broker?"

"Yes, sir."

"I don't understand what he wants of me, or how in the name of all that is curious he ever heard of me. I don't own any real estate, except a three-story house in which I live."

"Perhaps, sir, if you will go to the office with me you will get an explanation."

"Precisely. That is a very practical and sensible suggestion. Is it far off? I ask because I have never been in New York before."

"It is only about ten minutes' walk."

"Then I'll go with you, that is, if you can wait fifteen minutes while I finish writing a letter to my wife, apprising her of my safe arrival."

"Yes, sir, I am in no especial hurry."

"Then sit down, and—you may look at this," handing him the last copy of *Puck.*

Chester opened the paper eagerly, for *Puck* had accepted two of his sketches. He opened it at random, and his eye lighted up, for there was one of the two sketches handsomely reproduced. He uttered a little exclamation.

"What have you found?" asked Paul Perkins, looking up from his letter.

"This picture—is one of mine."

"You don't mean it!" exclaimed the man from Minneapolis, dropping his pen in surprise. "I thought you were an office boy."

"So I am, sir, but—sometimes I sell sketches to the illustrated papers."

"What did you get for this?"

"Seven dollars and a half. That is, I sold this and another for fifteen dollars."

"By the great horn spoon! but this is wonderful."

Chester did not feel called upon to say anything.

"How long did it take you to draw this picture?"

"A little over half an hour."

"Jerusalem! that is at the rate of ten dollars an hour. I am contented to make ten dollars a day."

"So should I be, sir. I don't draw all the time," said Chester, with a smile.

"I was going to ask if you wouldn't give me lessons in drawing and sketching."

"I should be afraid to, sir," laughed Chester. "You might prove a dangerous rival."

"You needn't be afraid. I can play as well as I can sing."

"I suppose you sing well, sir," said Chester, roguishly.

"You can judge. When I was a young man I thought I would practice singing a little in my room one night. The next morning my landlady said, in a tone of sympathy, 'I heard you groaning last night, Mr. Perkins. Did you have the toothache?'"

Chester burst into a hearty laugh.

"If that is the case," he said, "I won't be afraid of you as a rival in drawing."

Mr. Perkins set himself to finishing his letter, and in twenty minutes it was done.

"Now, I am ready," he said.

As they went downstairs, Chester observed, "I will ask you as a favor, Mr. Perkins, not to refer to my work in *Puck*, as it is not known at the office that I do any work outside."

"All right, my boy. By the way, how much do they pay you at the office?"

"Five dollars a week."

"Evidently it isn't as good a business as drawing."

"No, sir; but it is more reliable. I can't always satisfy the comic papers, and I am likely to have sketches left on my hands."

"Yes; that is a practical way of looking at it, and shows that you are a boy of sense. What sort of a man is Mr. Fairchild?"

"A very kind, considerate man, but I forgot to say that you won't see him."

"But I thought he sent you to call on me?"

"No, sir; Mr. Fairchild started for the West this morning. It was Mr. Mullins, the bookkeeper, who sent me."

"That complicates the mystery. Is he a good friend of yours?"

"No, sir; he dislikes me."

Mr. Perkins looked curious, and Chester, considerably to his own surprise, confided to him the story of his relations with the bookkeeper.

"He's a scamp!" commented the man from Minneapolis. "Why does Mr. Fairchild keep him. I wouldn't! I'd bounce him very quick."

"He has been with Mr. Fairchild five years and understands his business thoroughly."

"Well, there is something in that; but I wouldn't like to have in my employ a man whom I couldn't trust. Have you ever been out West?"

"No, sir."

"You ought to come out there. The city I represent is a smart one and no mistake. Of course you've heard of the rivalry between Minneapolis and St. Paul."

"Yes, sir."

"I don't take sides, for I live in both, but I think business facilities in Minneapolis are greater. I think you are a boy who would succeed at the West."

"I should like to go there some day. I own some property in

Washington Territory."

"You do?" exclaimed Paul Perkins, in great surprise. "Whereabouts?"

"In Tacoma. I own some lots there."

"Then let me tell you, my boy, that you will be a rich man."

"But I thought prices of land in Tacoma were small."

"So they are—at present; but it is the future terminus of the Northern Pacific Railroad. When it is completed there will be a boom. How many lots do you own?"

"Five."

"Take my advice and hold on to them. What square is this?"

They had reached Seventeenth Street.

"Union Square."

"It's a pretty place. Is Tiffany's near here?"

"Yes, sir; only two blocks away. We shall pass it."

"All right! Point it out to me. I'm going to buy a gold watch for myself there. I've needed one for a long time, but I wanted the satisfaction of buying one at Tiffany's. Anything that is sold there must be A No. 1."

"I have no doubt of it, but I don't trade there much yet."

"No; you must wait till you have realized on your Western lots."

They turned down Fourteenth Street, and soon stood in front of Mr. Fairchild's office. They entered, and this brings us to the point where the last chapter ends.

Horatio Alger, Jr

CHAPTER XXI

MR. PERKINS MAKES AN ACQUAINTANCE

Dick Ralston and the bookkeeper stared at their Western friend in undisguised amazement. Finally Mr. Mullins said, "What did I understand you to call yourself?"

"Paul Perkins, of Minneapolis."

"And—you are staying at the Fifth Avenue Hotel?"

"Certainly. Didn't you send this boy with a message?" said Mr. Perkins, rather impatiently.

"Ye-es."

"How did you know that I was coming to New York? That's what beats me."

Mullins began to appreciate the situation, and he was cudgeling his brains for an explanation. Finally one came.

"I may be misinformed, but I learned from a friend of yours that you were coming here with an intention of locating in our city. Now, as we are in the real estate business, I thought we would offer our services to find you a suitable house."

"Some friend of mine notified you of my coming to New York? Why, I started off on a sudden without consulting anyone. I don't see how anyone could give you the information."

"I won't undertake to explain it," said the bookkeeper. "I will only say that I am glad to meet you."

"Thank you! You are very polite. What was the name of the friend who spoke about me and my plans?"

"I have a poor memory for names, but I believe I have the gentleman's card in my desk."

He opened the desk and made an elaborate search for what he knew he should not find.

"It's no use," he said, after a pause. "It's disappeared."

"What was the appearance of the person?" persisted Mr. Perkins.

"He was—tall, and—yes, with a dark complexion and—and side whiskers."

"About how old?"

"I should say about forty."

"I know plenty of people answering that description. But how did he happen to call on you?"

"There you have me. He had some business with Mr. Fairchild, and unfortunately Mr. F. started West this morning."

"I see. I can get no clew to the mystery. However, I am glad to have made the acquaintance of this young man," indicating Chester.

"Oh, you mean our office boy," returned Mullins, coldly.

Just then Dick Ralston nudged the bookkeeper.

"Introduce me," he said, *sotto voce.*

The bookkeeper did not incline favorably to this request, but did not dare to refuse. Dick Ralston's appearance was decidedly against him, and his "loud" attire was in keeping with his face and manners.

"Mr. Perkins," said Mullins, "allow me to introduce my friend, Mr. Ralston."

"Glad to meet you, Mr. Ralston," said the man from Minneapolis, extending his hand, which Dick seized and pressed warmly.

"Proud to make your acquaintance, Mr. Perkins," rejoined the gambler. "I always did like Western people."

"Thank you. I am not Western by birth, though I went out to Minnesota when I was a mere boy."

"And I have no doubt you have prospered," said Ralston, who was really anxious to learn whether Mr. Perkins was well provided with money and was worth fleecing.

"Well, I don't complain," answered Perkins, in a matter-of-fact tone.

"I shall be glad to pay you any attentions," insinuated Ralston. "I know the ropes pretty well, and I flatter myself I can show you the town as well as anyone, eh, Mullins?"

"Oh, yes," assented the bookkeeper, not over cordially.

"I have no doubt of it, Mr. Ralston, and I take your offer kindly, but I am afraid I won't have time to go round much."

"Won't you go out and take a drink? Mullins, you go, too!"

"Thank you, but I don't drink—at any rate, when I am away from home. By the way, Mr.—" and he stopped short, for he did not remember the bookkeeper's name.

"Mr. Mullins," suggested that gentleman.

"You are misinformed about my wanting to locate in this city. New York's a right smart place, I admit, but give me Minneapolis. That suits me."

"All right, sir. I am misinformed, that's all."

"If you find my friend's card just write and let me know his name. I'd like to know who it is that knows so much about my plans."

"I will. Where shall I direct?"

"Oh, just direct to Minneapolis. I'm well known there. A letter will be sure to reach me."

"Shall you be at the hotel this evening, Mr. Perkins?" added Dick Ralston, who found it hard to give up his design upon his new acquaintance.

"I don't know. I haven't made any plans."

"I was thinking I might call upon you."

"Don't trouble yourself, Mr. Ralston. Probably you would not find me in."

Mr. Perkins was a tolerably shrewd man. He had "sized up" the gambler, and decided that he did not care to become any better acquainted with him.

"Just as you say," returned Dick Ralston, looking discomfited. "I thought perhaps I could make it pleasant for you."

"If I find I have time I can call at your place of business," said the man from Minneapolis, with a shrewd glance at the gambler.

"I have no place of business," returned Ralston, rather awkwardly. "I am a—a capitalist, and sometimes speculate in real estate. Don't I, Mullins?"

"Of course. By the way, I forgot to tell you that I have four lots on Ninety-sixth Street which would make a good investment."

"Ninety-sixth Street! Ahem, rather far uptown. What's the figure?"

"Five thousand dollars."

"I'll take a look at them as soon as I have time. You see, Mr. Perkins, I do all my real estate business through my friend, Mr. Mullins."

"Just so."

Neither Mr. Perkins nor Chester was taken in by Ralston's assumption of the character of a capitalist. The Western man had already a shrewd suspicion of the gambler's real business, and being a cautious and prudent man, did not care to cultivate him.

"Good-morning!" said Mr. Perkins. "I must not take up any more of your time. Will you allow Chester to go out with me for five minutes?"

"Certainly."

David Mullins would have liked to refuse, but had no good excuse for doing so.

"Don't stay long!" he said, rather sharply.

"I won't keep him long."

When they were in the street Mr. Perkins said: "I don't like the looks of that bookkeeper of yours."

"Nor do I," returned Chester.

"I wouldn't trust him any further than I could see him. Who was that Ralston? Have you ever seen him before?"

"Once. He doesn't come into the office when Mr. Fairchild is at home."

"Do you know anything about him?"

"I know—that is, I have heard that he is a well-known gambler."

"By the great horn spoon, if I didn't think so! He seemed

very anxious to show me round the city."

"He would probably have taken you to a gambling house."

"Not if I was in my senses. I don't gamble, and I hope you don't."

"I shouldn't know how," answered Chester, with a smile.

"Have you any engagement for this evening?"

"No, sir."

"What time do you leave the office?"

"At five o'clock."

"Then come round to the hotel and take dinner with me. I don't know anyone in the city, and I shall be glad to have your company this evening. We will take a walk together, and you can show me what's worth seeing."

"Are you not afraid that I will take you to a gambling house?" asked Chester, with a smile.

"I'll risk it."

"You would find Mr. Ralston a better guide."

"But not so safe a one. I shall be satisfied with you."

When Chester returned to the office Mullins asked, sharply: "What did Perkins want to say to you?"

"He asked me to dine with him to-night at the Fifth Avenue Hotel."

"Speak a good word for me, Chester," said Ralston, with unusual affability. "I would like to become better acquainted with him."

"What shall I say, Mr. Ralston?"

"Tell him I am a prominent man, and expect to be nominated for Congress next fall."

This he said with a wink. Chester and the bookkeeper laughed.

"I'll tell him," said Chester.

CHAPTER XXII

DICK RALSTON'S FATHER

When Chester followed Mr. Perkins into the great dining room of the Fifth Avenue he was rather dazzled by its size and the glistening appearance of the tables.

"I hope you have brought your appetite with you, Chester," said his Western friend. "The Fifth Avenue sets a good table."

"My appetite is sure to be good. I was kept so busy to-day that I had hardly time to buy a sandwich for lunch."

"All the better! You'll enjoy your meal. As for me, I don't have the appetite I do at home. There's nothing like a tramp on the open prairie to make a man feel peckish."

"Have you ever been in New York before, Mr. Perkins?"

"Not since I was a boy. I was born up Albany way, and came here when I was about your age. But, Lord, the New York of that day wasn't a circumstance to what it is now. There was no Elevated railroad then, nor horse cars either, for that matter, and where this hotel stands there was a riding school or something of that sort."

"Are you going to stay here long?"

"I go to Washington to-morrow, stopping at Philadelphia and Baltimore on the way. No. I have no business in Washington, but I think by the time a man is fifty odd he ought to see the capital of his country. I shall shake hands with the President, too, if I find him at home."

"Have you ever been further West than Minneapolis?"

"Yes, I have been clear out to the Pacific. I've seen the town of Tacoma, where you've got five lots. I shall write out to a friend in Portland to buy me as many. Then we shall both have an interest there."

"You think the lots are worth something?"

"I know it. When the Northern Pacific Railroad is finished, every dollar your friend spent for his lots will be worth thirty or forty."

"I hope your predictions will come true, Mr. Perkins."

"Did I hear you speaking of Tacoma?" asked a gentleman on Chester's left hand.

"Yes, sir."

"I can tell you something about it. I live at Seattle."

"Am I right about there being a future for the place?" asked Paul Perkins.

"You are. I may say that lots there are already worth twice what they were last week."

"How's that?"

"Because work on the railroad has been resumed, and there is no doubt now that it will be pushed to completion."

"That settles it. I must own property there. I won't wait to write, but will telegraph my friend in Portland to go there at once at my expense, and buy five—no, ten lots. I got that idea from you, Chester, and if I make a profit I shall feel indebted to you."

"I shall be glad if it helps fill your pockets, Mr. Perkins."

"Come up to my room for a while, Chester," went on the other, "and we will consider what to do. We might go to the theater, but I think I would rather walk about here and there using my eyes. There is plenty to see in New York."

"That will suit me, Mr. Perkins."

About eight o'clock the two went downstairs. Near the entrance, just inside the hotel, Chester heard himself called by name.

Looking up, he recognized Felix Gordon.

"Are you going to the theater, Chester?" asked Felix.

"No, I think not."

"Won't you introduce me to your friend?"

"Mr. Perkins, this is Felix Gordon, nephew of our book-keeper," said Chester, unwillingly.

"Hope you are well, Mr. Gordon," said Paul. "Are you fond

of the theater?"

"Yes, sir," answered Felix, eagerly. "There's a good play at Palmer's. I think you'd like it."

"No doubt, but I'd rather see the streets of New York. As you are a friend of Chester, do me the favor to buy yourself a ticket," and Mr. Perkins drew a two-dollar bill from his pocket and tendered it to Felix.

"I am ever so much obliged," said Felix, effusively. "As it is time for the performance to commence, I'll go at once, if you'll excuse me."

"Certainly. You don't want to lose the beginning of the play."

As Felix started off on a half run, Mr. Perkins said: "Do you know why I was so polite to Felix, who by all accounts isn't your friend at all?"

"No, I was rather puzzled."

"I wanted to get rid of him. He was probably sent here by his uncle as a spy upon us. Now he is disposed of."

"I see you are shrewd," said Chester, laughing.

"Yes, I'm a little foxy when there's occasion," rejoined Mr. Perkins. "Now, where shall we go?"

I will not undertake to describe the route followed by the two. The city was pretty much all new to the stranger from Minneapolis, and it mattered little where he went.

About ten o'clock the two witnessed from a distance a scene between a man of forty and an old, infirm man, apparently seventy years of age.

"The younger man is Ralston, the gambler," said Chester, in excitement, when they were near enough to recognize the figures of the two.

"Halt a minute, and let us hear what it is all about," returned Mr. Perkins.

"I am hungry," said the old man, pitifully, "and I have no money for a bed. Have pity on me, Dick, and give me something."

"You ought not to have come here," returned Ralston, roughly. "Why didn't you stay in the country, where you had a comfortable home?"

"In the poorhouse," murmured the old man, sadly.

"Well, it's no worse for being a poorhouse, is it?"

"But is it right for me to live there when you are rich and prosperous?"

"How do you know I am rich and prosperous?"

"By your dress. And there's a diamond in your shirt bosom. That must be valuable."

"It's about all I own that is valuable. It was a fool's errand that brought you here. You had better go back," and Ralston prepared to go on.

"Won't you give me a trifle, Dick?"

"Well, take that."

"A quarter?"

"Yes; it will give you some supper."

"But what shall I do for a bed?"

"Go to the station house. They'll take in an old man like you."

Before the aged man could renew his application the younger one had disappeared round the corner of the next street.

"Follow me, Chester," said Paul Perkins. "I'm going to speak to the old man."

He touched him on the shoulder.

"Are you in trouble, my friend?" he asked.

The old man, looking the picture of despondency in his ragged suit, and with his long, gray locks floating over his shoulders, turned at the words.

"Yes, sir," he said, "I am poor and in trouble, and my heart is sore."

"Is the man who has just left you related to you?"

"He is my only son."

"He doesn't seem kind to you."

"No; he cares nothing for his old father."

"How did you become so poor?"

"He is the cause. When he was turned twenty-one I was worth ten thousand dollars. He forged my name, more than once, and to save him I paid the forged notes. So it happened that I was turned out in my old age from the farm and the home that had been mine for twenty-five years, and in the end I was sent to the poorhouse."

"Then he brought all this upon you?"

"Yes."

"Do you know what he is now?"

"He tells me he is in business."

"His business is carried on at the gambling house, so my young friend here assures me. You will get no help from him."

"I begin to think so. Perhaps I was foolish to leave my home, poor as it was, and come here to ask help."

"How much money will take you home?"

"Two dollars."

"Here is a ten-dollar bill. Take it, get a meal and a night's lodging and in the morning start for home. It is the best thing you can do. As for your son, you can only leave him to his own devices. A man who will treat his old father as he has treated you will never prosper."

"Thank you, sir. I will follow your advice."

"I would rather be in your position, old and poor as you are, than in his."

"Chester," added Mr. Perkins, as they walked on, "this Ralston is a more contemptible rascal than I thought. If my old father were living, I would give half the money I possess. While I had a dollar in my pocket he should share it."

"I say the same, Mr. Perkins."

When they reached the Fifth Avenue Hotel, Paul Perkins shook hands with Chester.

"Good-night," he said. "You won't see me for two weeks, perhaps, but I'll be sure to find you out when I return to the city. I hope you won't have any trouble with that scoundrel in the office."

"Thank you, Mr. Perkins, but I am afraid I shall."

"Don't mind it if you do. Remember that you will always have a friend in Paul Perkins."

CHAPTER XXIII

CHESTER IS DISCHARGED

"Well," said David Mullins, addressing his cousin Felix, "did you go to the Fifth Avenue Hotel last evening?"

"Yes, Cousin David."

"Did you see that man from Minneapolis and Chester?"

"Yes."

"Where did they go?"

"I don't know."

"You don't know?" frowned Mullins. "And why not, I should like to know?"

"Because I went to Palmer's Theater."

"So that is the way you spent the quarter I gave you?" exclaimed the bookkeeper, indignantly.

"I couldn't go to Palmer's on that."

"Did you go with them?" asked Mullins, hopefully.

"No, but Mr. Perkins gave me money to go."

"What made him do it?"

"He thought I was a friend of Chester."

"How much did he give you?"

"I occupied a dollar seat," answered Felix, noncommittally.

He did not care to mention that the sum given him was two dollars, half of which he still had in his pocket.

"Humph! so he gave you a dollar. Why didn't you take it and stay with them?"

"Because he gave it to me expressly for the theater. It would have looked strange if I had stayed with them after all."

"I would have found a way, but you are not smart."

Felix did not make any reply, being content with having deceived his cousin as to Mr. Perkins' gift.

"I say, Cousin David, aren't you going to bounce that boy pretty quick and give me his place?"

"Yes, as soon as I get a good excuse."

"Will you do it to-day?"

"No; it would look strange. You may be sure I won't keep him long."

At this point Chester came into the office and was surprised to see Mr. Mullins and Felix already there. Usually the bookkeeper did not show up till half an hour later.

"Good-morning," said Mullins, smoothly. "Did you dine with Mr. Perkins last evening?"

"Yes, sir."

"I suppose you went to the theater?"

"No; Mr. Perkins preferred to take a walk, as he has not been in New York since he was a boy. Did you enjoy the play, Felix?"

"Yes, thank you. It was very nice. I am ever so much obliged to Mr. Perkins for the money to go."

"Mr. Perkins must be a rich man?" said Mullins, interrogatively.

"I think he is pretty well off," answered Chester.

"How long does he stay in the city?"

"He was to leave this morning. He is going to Washington."

David Mullins was glad to hear this. It would make it easier for him to discharge Chester.

He dispatched him on an errand, and was about to make some entries in the books when Dick Ralston strolled in.

"How are you, Dick? Can I do anything for you this morning?"

"Yes; you can let me have a hundred dollars."

"I can't do that," answered the bookkeeper, with a slight frown.

"You'll have to settle up soon," said Ralston, in a surly tone.

"Give me time, can't you? I can't do everything in a minute. What is the matter with you? You look as if you had got out of the wrong side of the bed."

"I had a disagreeable thing happen last evening. Who should appear to me on Madison Avenue but the old man."

"Your father?"

"Yes; he left a good, comfortable home up in the country, and came here to see if he couldn't get some money out of me."

"Did he?"

"I gave him a quarter and advised him to go back. He seems to think I am made of money."

"So he has a comfortable home?"

"Yes," answered Ralston, hesitating slightly. "He's better off than I am in one way. He has no board to pay, and sometimes I haven't money to pay mine."

"I suppose he is staying with friends or relatives," said Mullins, who was not aware that Mr. Ralston, senior, was the inmate of a poorhouse.

"It is an arrangement I made for him. I felt angry to see him here, and I told him so. However, he isn't likely to come again. Have you heard from Fairchild yet?"

"No; it isn't time. He won't reach Chicago till this evening or to-morrow morning."

"Meanwhile—that is, while he is away—you have full swing, eh?"

"Yes; I suppose so."

"Then you'll be a fool if you don't take advantage of it."

David Mullins did not answer. He repented, now that it was too late, that he had placed himself in the power of such a man as Dick Ralston. As long as he owed him seven hundred and fifty dollars there was no escaping him, and Mullins felt very uncomfortable when he considered what steps the gambler wanted him to take to get free from his debts.

At this moment a dignified-looking gentleman living on West Forty-seventh Street entered the office. He was the owner of a large building, of which Mr. Fairchild acted as agent. He looked askance at Dick Ralston, whose loud dress and general appearance left little doubt as to his character.

"Is Mr. Fairchild in?" the caller asked.

"No, sir; he started for the West yesterday."

"I am sorry."

"I can attend to your business, Mr. Gray."

"No, thank you. I prefer to wait. How long will Mr. Fairchild be absent?"

"Probably six weeks."

The gentleman took his leave, with another side glance at Ralston.

When he had gone, Ralston said, "Who is that, Mullins?"

"Mr. Gray, a wealthy banker, living on Forty-seventh Street."

"So? Why didn't you introduce me to the old duffer? I might have made something out of him."

"He is not your style, Dick. He wouldn't care to be introduced to a stranger."

"So he puts on airs, does he?"

"No; but he is rather a proud, reserved man."

"Thinks himself better than his fellow men, I suppose," sneered the gambler.

"I can't say, but it wouldn't have been policy to make you acquainted. If you won't be offended, Dick, I will say that though I am personally your friend, I am afraid that it isn't best for you to be here so much."

"So you are getting on your high horse, Mullins, are you?"

"No; but you are too well known, Dick. If you were only an ordinary man, now, it would be different, but your striking appearance naturally makes people curious about you."

Dick Ralston was not insensible to flattery, and this compliment propitiated him. He was about to go out when Chester entered, returning from his errand.

"How are you, kid?" inquired Ralston.

"Very well, Mr. Ralston," answered Chester, coldly, for he could not forget how the gambler had treated his old father.

"Well, did you pass the evening with that cowboy from Minneapolis?"

"I spent the evening with Mr. Perkins."

"Of course! That's what I mean. Has he got money?"

"He didn't tell me."

"He gave Felix money to go to the theater," interposed Mullins.

"Is that so? He seems to be liberal. I'd like to cultivate his acquaintance. How long is he going to stay at the Fifth Avenue?"

"He left for Washington this morning."

"I am sorry to hear it. Another chance gone, Mullins."

The bookkeeper looked warningly at Ralston. He did not care to have him speak so freely before the office boy.

"I don't suppose we are likely to have any business with Paul Perkins," he said. "I offered to sell him a house, but he doesn't care to locate in New York."

Things went on as usual for the rest of the day. Mr. Mullins, if anything, treated Chester better than usual, and the office boy began to think that he had done the bookkeeper injustice. Felix spent considerable of his time in the office, spending his time in reading nickel libraries, of which he generally carried a supply with him.

On the next day, about three o'clock in the afternoon, Chester was sent downtown on an errand. He was delayed about ten minutes by a block on the Sixth Avenue car line. When he entered the office, Mullins demanded, sharply, "What made you so long?"

Chester explained.

"That's too thin!" retorted the bookkeeper. "I have no doubt you loitered, wasting your employer's time."

"That isn't true, Mr. Mullins," said Chester, indignantly.

"You won't mend mattters by impertinence. It is clear to me that you won't suit us. I will pay you your wages up to this evening, and you can look for another place."

"Mr. Fairchild engaged me, Mr. Mullins. It is only right that you should keep me till he returns, and report your objections."

"I don't require any instructions from you. You are discharged—do you understand?"

"Yes," answered Chester, slowly.

"You needn't wait till evening. Here is your money. Felix will take your place for the present."

"Yes, Cousin David," returned Felix, with alacrity.

"I protest against this sudden discharge," said Chester, "for no fault of my own, Mr. Mullins."

"You have said enough. I understand my business."

There was nothing for Chester to do but to accept the dismissal. It took him by surprise, for though he anticipated ill treatment, he had not expected to be discharged.

"Well, Felix," said the bookkeeper, "you've got the place at last."

"Yes," smiled Felix, complacently. "Didn't Chester look glum when you bounced him?"

"I don't know and I don't care. I have no further use for him. He's too fresh!"

CHAPTER XXIV

INTRODUCES MR. SHARPLEIGH, THE DETECTIVE

Chester was not so much disturbed by his discharge, so far as it related to his own welfare, as by the thought that Mr. Fairchild's interests were threatened. He felt that his absent employer ought to be notified at once.

Accordingly he went to the Fifth Avenue Hotel and telegraphed to Chicago:

"I am discharged. Felix Gordon is in my place. Will write."

A few hours later Chester received the following message at his lodgings.

"Your telegram received. Will write you instructions. FAIRCHILD."

Two days later Chester received a letter requesting him to call at once on a well-known detective, give him all the available information and request him to keep careful watch of Mr. Mullins and his operations, and interfere if any steps were taken prejudicial to Mr. Fairchild's interests.

Chester called on the detective and was fortunate enough to find him in. He expected to see a large man of impressive manners and imposing presence, and was rather disappointed when he found a small personage under the average height, exceedingly plain and unpretentious, who might easily have been taken for an humble clerk on a salary of ten or twelve dollars a week.

Mr. Sharpleigh listened attentively to Chester's communication, and then proceeded to ask questions.

"Do you know anything of Mr. Mullins outside of the office?" he asked.

"A little, sir."

"Has he any bad habits? Is he extravagant? Does he drink?"

"I have never seen any evidence that he drank," answered Chester. "Perhaps he may drink a glass of wine or beer occasionally."

"I don't mean that. He is not what may be called an intemperate man?"

"No, sir."

"Any other objectionable habits?"

"I think he gambles."

"Ha! this is important. What makes you think so?"

"He seems to be intimate with a man who, I am told, is a well-known gambler."

"Who is it?"

"Dick Ralston."

"Ralston is as well known as any gambler in the city. How is it that this has not excited the suspicions of Mr. Fairchild?"

"I don't think Mr. Fairchild knows it."

"Then Ralston doesn't come into the office?"

"He did not when Mr. Fairchild was in town. As soon as Mr. Fairchild left he came at once, and now spends considerable time there."

"Probably Mullins owes him money lost in gambling."

"I think he does. I overheard him one day urging Mr. Mullins to give him money."

"That makes it probable. Do you know if they keep company outside?"

"I have seen them walking late in the evening."

"Why do you think Mr. Mullins discharged you?"

"He wanted the place for a cousin of his."

"What name?"

"Felix Gordon."

"Is he there now?"

"Yes; Felix was taken on when I was discharged."

"At once?"

"Yes. He was in the office, probably waiting for the vacancy."

"The plan seems to have been cut and dried. What sort of a boy is Felix?"

"I don't know him very well. He seems on confidential terms with Mr. Mullins."

"Did the bookkeeper have any other reasons for disliking you?"

"Yes; I interfered to prevent his cheating a mechanic out of his month's rent."

"State the circumstances."

Chester did so.

"How long has Mr. Mullins been in Mr. Fairchild's employ?"

"About five years, I think I have heard."

"That speaks well for him. Probably his acquaintance with Ralston is recent, or he would have done something before this to insure his discharge."

There was a short silence, and Chester asked: "Have you any more questions, Mr. Sharpleigh?"

"Not at present. Will you give me your address?"

Chester did so.

"I will send for you if I need you. I think you can help me materially. You seem to have a clear head, and are observing."

It was the evening for Chester to call at Prof. Hazlitt's.

"I passed your office this morning, Chester," said Arthur Burks, "and thought of calling in, but I was in haste."

"You wouldn't have found me, Arthur. I am discharged."

"What!" exclaimed Arthur, in surprise. "What complaint does Mr. Fairchild make of you?"

"None at all. He is out of the city. The bookkeeper, who dislikes me, discharged me, and gave the place to his cousin."

"I am awfully sorry. What will you do?"

"I have some money saved up. Besides, I shall devote more time to drawing. I made a sketch yesterday which Mr. Conrad thinks I will get ten dollars for."

"That is fine. I never earned ten dollars in my life."

"You have never felt obliged to work, except in school."

"I take care not to injure my health in studying," said Arthur, with a laugh.

"I will speak to uncle Edgar, and he will arrange to have you come four times a week instead of two. Then you will earn more money from him."

"Thank you, Arthur. I should like that."

Prof. Hazlitt, on being spoken to, ratified this arrangement, so that Chester's mind was easy. He knew now that he would be able to support himself and more, too.

Chester soon had something more to encourage him. He received at his lodgings the following letter:

"MR. CHESTER RAND.

"DEAR SIR: We are about to establish a new comic weekly, which we shall call *The Phoenix*. It is backed by sufficient capital to insure its success. Our attention has been called to some illustrations which you have furnished to some of our successful contemporaries, and we shall be glad to secure your services. We may be able to throw considerable work in your way. Please call at our office as soon as possible.

"EDITORS OF THE PHOENIX."

Chester was quite exhilarated by this letter. He felt that it was a proof of his growing popularity as an artist, and this was particularly gratifying. Besides, his income would be largely, at any rate considerably, increased. He lost no time in presenting himself at the office of *The Phoenix*.

It was located in a large office building on Nassau Street. He took the elevator and went upstairs to the sixth floor. On the door of a room a little way from the elevator he saw the name, and knocked.

"Come in!" was the response.

Chester opened the door and found himself in the presence of a man of about forty, with a profusion of brown hair shading a pleasant countenance. He looked up inquiringly as

Chester entered.

"Is this the editor of *The Phoenix*?" inquired Chester, respectfully.

"*The Phoenix* will have no existence till next week," answered the other, pleasantly. "I expect to be its editor."

"I came in answer to your letter."

"To my letter?" repeated the editor, puzzled.

"Yes; my name is Chester Rand."

"What!" exclaimed the brown-haired man, almost incredulously. "You—a boy? How old are you?"

"Sixteen."

"And you are a contributor to *Puck* and other papers?"

"Yes, sir."

"You must be a smart boy. Shake hands."

Chester shook hands with a smile.

"Will my being a boy make any difference?" he asked.

"Not if your work is satisfactory. Are you willing to work exclusively for *The Phoenix*?"

"Yes, sir; that is, if I may be allowed to complete a contract I have made."

"What sort of a contract?"

"I am illustrating Prof. Hazlitt's ethnological work. I think it may take me some months more, working evenings."

"That won't interfere with us. I was afraid you might be under an engagement with a rival publication."

"No, sir. So far as that goes I will confine myself to *The Phoenix* if—"

"Terms are satisfactory, I suppose."

"Yes, sir."

"Then I will agree to pay you twenty-five dollars a week for the first six months. I may be able to do better afterward."

Chester was dazzled. Twenty-five dollars a week! What would Silas Tripp say to that or his enemy, the bookkeeper.

"I accept," he answered, promptly.

CHAPTER XXV

CHESTER MEETS ANOTHER ARTIST

"Where do you wish me to work?" asked Chester, after a pause.

"You can work at home, but you can call at the office every day to leave your work and receive instructions."

"All right, sir. When do you wish me to commence?"

"At once. Have you any work ready? I asked because we want to get out the first number as soon as possible."

"I have one sketch and have several ideas jotted down."

"Good! Deliver as much as possible to-morrow."

Chester returned home in a high state of exultation. He would be paid less for individual sketches, but, on the other hand, he would have a steady income and an assured market for all he might produce. It seemed a wonderful promotion from five dollars a week to twenty-five. To be sure, when in the real estate office he had picked up extra compensation for outside work, but this was precarious and could not be depended on. With twenty-five dollars a week he would feel rich. This set him to considering that he must have a better room if he was to do work at home. In the same house where he now occupied a hall bedroom was a large, square room well lighted with two windows, well furnished and having a good writing desk, left by some previous tenant in part payment of arrears of rent, which he could have for five dollars a week. He had often thought he would like to occupy it, and wished he might find an agreeable roommate who would share the expense with him. Now he felt that he could bear the expense alone. He lost no time in securing it and moving his few belongings in.

Mrs. Crosby, his landlady, was rather surprised.

"You must be doing well," she said.

Chester smiled.

"I have been discharged from my position in the real estate office," he said.

"Then," said the landlady, in some dismay, "isn't it impru-dent to take a more expensive room?"

"I have secured a much better place."

"Oh! that alters the case. Is it likely to be permanent?"

"If I lose it I will go back to my old room."

"I am sure I am glad to hear of your good luck, Mr. Rand. It is very seldom that a young man of your age—"

"Call me a boy. I am not a young man yet."

"You seem to be getting on as well as a young man. I think

you are real smart."

"You mustn't flatter me, Mrs. Crosby. You will make me vain. I forgot to say that I shall be a considerable part of the time in my room. That is why I want a larger one."

"But when will you work?" asked the landlady, puzzled.

"I shall work in my room."

"But what work can you do there?"

"I am an artist; that is, I am to make drawings for a new magazine."

"You don't say so? Will that pay?"

"Very handsomely."

"I hope you will show me some of them. I never met an artist before."

"I am afraid I am not much of an artist. I can show you one of my pictures now."

Chester took from the table a number of *Puck* and pointed out a sketch.

"That's pretty good," said the landlady. "You wouldn't get more than thirty-five cents for such a picture, would you?"

"I was paid five dollars for that."

"Do tell!" exclaimed Mrs. Crosby, who was brought up in a country town and still used some of the expressions which were familiar to her in early days. "I can't hardly believe it. It seems foolish to pay so much for such a little thing."

"I don't think it foolish, Mrs. Crosby. It must pay them, or they wouldn't keep on doing it."

Chester moved into his new room and enjoyed his ample accommodations very much. The next day he went to the office of *The Phoenix* and carried in two sketches. They were fortunate enough to win the approval of the editor.

"I see you are practical and understand what we want, Mr. Rand," he said. Just behind Chester was a man of fifty, rather shabby and neglectful in his personal appearance. He might be described as an artist going to seed. Whatever talent he might have had originally had been dulled and obscured by chronic intemperance.

"Excuse me, sir," he said, deferentially, "but I would like to submit a couple of sketches. I am Guy Radcliff."

"Glad to see you, Mr. Radcliff. Let me examine them."

"I am afraid," said the editor, after a brief examination, "that these are not quite what we want."

"Is it possible?" exclaimed Mr. Radcliff, indignantly. "You scorn my work, yet accept the sketches of that boy!" pointing at Chester with withering contempt.

"Because he has given me what I want."

"I was a famous artist before he was born."

"Very likely, and had done good work. But this is not good work."

"Sir!"

"My dear sir, don't be offended. I don't care for the age of any of my contributors. I know something of your famous successes, and I hope next time to approve and buy what you bring me."

Mr. Radcliff seemed only half propitiated. He and Chester went out together.

"What is your name, boy?" asked the artist.

"Chester Rand."

"I never heard of you."

"I am only a beginner," said Chester, modestly.

"You seem to have got in with Fleming."

"I may not keep in with him."

"Are you doing pretty well?"

"Yes, for a boy."

"Have you got a loose quarter about you? I haven't done much work lately, and am hard up."

Chester took half a dollar from his pocket and handed it to the elder man. His compassion was stirred as he felt for Radcliff's humiliation in being obliged to make such an appeal to a boy like himself.

"Thank you. You're a gentleman. I'll return it soon," said Radcliff, looking relieved. "Good luck to you! You're a good fellow, after all."

"I wish you good luck, too, Mr. Radcliff."

Chester did not need to be told what had brought the elder artist into such an impecunious condition. His face with its unnatural flush showed that his habits had been far from creditable.

"If I needed anything to keep me from drinking, Mr. Radcliff's example would be sufficient," thought Chester. He had before now been invited to take a drink at some convenient saloon, but he had never been tempted to do so.

Two days later Chester was walking through Union Square when he came face to face with Felix Gordon.

Felix espied him first.

"Hello! Chester," said his successor.

"Hello! I didn't see you."

"I envy you."

"Why?"

"You have nothing to do but to enjoy yourself," answered Felix, significantly.

"Oh, that's it!" said Chester, smiling. He saw that Felix thought him to be out of employment.

"That was the case with you before you succeeded me in the real estate office. How do you like it?"

"Pretty well, but I think I ought to get more salary. You got five dollars, didn't you?"

"Yes."

"I will try and get six when Mr. Fairchild gets back."

"I wish you success."

"You don't feel any grudge against me for taking your place?"

"No; it wasn't you who got me discharged."

"I thought you'd be in to get a letter of recommendation from cousin David."

"Would he give me one?"

"I don't know. Are you trying to get a place?"

"No."

Felix looked surprised.

"You ain't rich, are you?" he asked.

"No; what makes you ask?"

"I don't see how you can live without any salary."

"I couldn't. I ought to tell you that I have got a place."

"You have?" exclaimed Felix, in surprise, and it must be confessed, disappointment.

"Yes."

"Where is it?"

"In the office of a new paper."

"What is it?"

"*The Phoenix*, a comic paper just started."

"Where is the office?"

"In Nassau Street."

"Then why are you not there?"

"I don't have to be there all the time."

"Do you get good pay?"

"Yes."

"How much?"

"I get more than I did at the real estate office."

"You don't say!"

"Yes. I was in luck."

"Do you get six dollars?"

"More. I don't care to tell you just how much I get."

"By the way, there was an old man in the office yesterday inquiring after you."

"Did he give his name?"

"Yes. He said his name was Silas Tripp."

"What on earth brought Mr. Tripp to New York?" Chester asked himself.

This question will be answered in the next chapter.

CHAPTER XXVI

A STRANGER IN NEW YORK

It was not often that Silas Tripp went to New York. The expense was a consideration, and again he found it difficult to leave his business. But he had received a circular from an investment company in Wall Street, offering ten per cent. interest for any money he might have to invest. High interest always attracts men who love money, and it so happened that Silas had five hundred dollars invested. The difference between six and ten per cent. interest on this sum would make twenty dollars annually, besides a contingent share in extra profits promised in the circular, and on the whole he thought it would pay him to make the journey.

He went at once to the office of Messrs. Gripp & Co., on his arrival in the city. He found the financial agents occupying handsome offices, well furnished and covered with a thick Turkey carpet. Everything betokened prosperity, and Mr. Tripp was dazzled. The result was that he made the investment and laid away in his old-fashioned wallet five new bonds, assuring a dividend of ten per cent.

"I calc'late it's safe," he said to Mr. Gripp, a stout man with a florid face, expensively dressed and sporting a large and showy diamond ring.

"Assuredly, my dear sir," said Gripp, with suavity. "I congratulate you, Mr. Tripp, on making an unusually profitable investment. I venture to say that within the year, besides the regular dividend, there will be an extra dividend of five per cent., making fifteen per cent. in all. It is a pity you had not more invested."

"Mebby I'll bring you in some more bimeby," said Mr. Tripp, cautiously.

"I trust you will, for your own sake. To us it is not important, as we have plenty of capital offered. Indeed, we have had to limit investments to five thousand dollars for each person. Why, a millionaire, whose name would be very familiar to you if I could venture to mention it, came here last week and wanted to invest fifty thousand dollars in our bonds, but I firmly refused to take more than five thousand."

"I don't see why you should," said Silas, puzzled.

"I will tell you why. We wish to give a chance to smaller investors, like yourself, for instance. Rich men have plenty of ways in which to invest their money to advantage, while you probably don't know where to get over six per cent."

"No; I never got more'n that."

"I dare say you have considerable invested at that small interest."

"Well, mebbe."

"Think how much it would be for your advantage to get four per cent. more."

"To be sure, sartin! Well, I'll think of it, Mr. Gripp. Mebbe

I'll come and see you ag'in soon."

Mr. Gripp smiled to himself. He saw that the bait was likely to prove effective.

"Well, good-by, Mr. Gripp. You'll send me any information about the bonds?"

"Yes, Mr. Tripp, with pleasure. Whenever you are in the city, even if you have no business with us, make our office your home. Whenever you have any letters to write, we will furnish you a desk and all facilities."

"Thank you, Mr. Gripp; you're very obleeging."

So the old man went out, feeling very complacent over his new investment, and much pleased with the handsome way he was treated by Mr. Gripp.

"Lemme see," he reflected. "I've got five thousand dollars invested. At ten per cent. it would amount to five hundred dollars, and with an extra dividend of two hundred and fifty dollars more. I'll have to think it over. All seems safe and square, and Mr. Gripp is a real gentleman."

Silas Tripp looked at his watch. It was only half-past ten. How should he occupy his spare time?

"I guess I'll go and see Chester Rand," he said. "His mother told me where he was working. Perhaps he'll know of some cheap place where I can get dinner. The last time I was in the city it cost me forty cents. That's a terrible price."

Mr. Tripp knew the location of Mr. Fairchild's office, and after some inquiry he found his way there. He felt so much like a stranger in the big city that he anticipated with pleasure seeing a familiar face. Perhaps Chester would invite him out to lunch, and Mr. Tripp, in his frugality, would not have declined the offer even of an office boy, as long as it would save him expense.

Felix Gordon was just leaving the office on an errand.

"Is that Mr. Fairchild's office?" inquired Silas.

"Yes," answered Felix, with rather a disdainful glance at Silas Tripp's rusty garments.

"Much obleeged to ye," said Silas.

He entered the office and glanced about, expecting to see Chester.

David Mullins came forward, and with some show of civility greeted the old country merchant. Though he was not naturally polite, he knew that the size of a man's purse could not always be judged from the cut or quality of his garments, and he was just as ready to make money out of Silas as out of any fashionably dressed customer.

"Is Mr. Fairchild in?" asked Silas.

"No; Mr. Fairchild is out West. I am Mr. Mullins, his bookkeeper, and represent him."

"Just so! Have you a boy workin' for you named Chester— Chester Rand?"

"Are you a friend of his?" asked the bookkeeper.

"Well, yes. I come from Wyncombe, where he lives, and I know his folks. I was told he was workin' here."

"Yes, he was working here," answered Mullins, emphasizing the past tense.

"Isn't he here now?" demanded Silas, with surprise.

"No."

"How's that?"

"It's rather a delicate matter, as you are a friend of his, but some days since I was obliged to discharge him."

"You don't say!" ejaculated Silas, in manifest surprise.

"I am sorry to say it."

"But what was the matter? What did he do?"

"Well, as to that, he did nothing very serious, but he wasted time when he was sent out on an errand, and I felt that it was injurious to the interests of Mr. Fairchild to retain him."

"He used to be spry enough when he worked for me."

"When he worked for you?"

"Yes. I keep a store out in Wyncombe, and he was in my employ most a year. I used to think him quite a lively boy."

"I dare say he would do very well in a country store, but in the city we want boys to be active and wide awake. I don't want to say anything against him. He was perfectly honest, so far as I know."

"Has he got another place?"

"I don't think he has. It is difficult for a boy to get a place in this city—that is, a good place, and he wouldn't be likely to refer any employer to me."

"I'm afraid he'll be put to it to live, for his mother was poor. How much wages did you pay him?"

"Five dollars a week."

"That's pretty high pay."

"So it is, and we expect a first-class boy for that."

"Have you got a better boy in his place?"

"Yes; I have taken in a cousin of mine who knows my ways and satisfies me."

"Was it the boy I saw just after I came in—a dark-complexioned boy with black hair?"

"Yes, that is Felix."

"And you find him better than Chester?"

"Yes."

Silas Tripp did not make any comments, but he had not been very favorably impressed by the little he had seen of Chester's successor.

"Mebbe Chester isn't adapted to the city," Silas said.

"I think you are right. It would be better for him to go back into your store, but country boys fancy they must come to the city and become city business men."

"That's so. Mebbe I wouldn't succeed in the city myself, though I'm doin' a tidy business in Wyncombe. I'd like to see Chester. Can you tell me where he lives?"

"No, I haven't his address."

"I wonder he hasn't gone back home. Mebbe he hasn't got the money."

"I presume you are correct in your conjecture."

"His mother hasn't said anything to me about Chester bein' out of work. I'm surprised at that."

"Perhaps he did not like to tell her."

"Very like, very like! I'm really sorry to hear Chester ain't done no better."

"He isn't quite up to our mark, but I dare say he will do very well in the country or in some small business."

"Are you doin' a large business? You don't seem to have much stock here."

"My dear sir, we can't get brownstone houses and country villas into an office like this."

"Is that what you sell?"

"Yes; I sold a fifty-thousand-dollar house this morning up on Forty-fifth Street, and yesterday I sold a summer hotel for forty thousand dollars. Our commission in each case would be several hundred dollars."

"Sho! Well, you be doin' a good business. Can you tell where

I can get a good dinner moderate?"

Felix came in at this moment.

"Felix," said his cousin, "you may keep the office while I go out to lunch. Mr.—You didn't tell me your name."

"Silas Tripp."

"Mr. Tripp, it will give me pleasure if you will go out and take lunch with me."

"Well, I am sure you're very polite," said Silas, pleased to think he would be saved expense; "I'm much obliged."

So the two went out together. Mullins continued to say considerable that was derogatory to Chester, and left Mr. Tripp under the impression that he was a failure so far as New York business was concerned.

CHAPTER XXVII

MR. TRIPP IS DISAPPOINTED

Silas Tripp returned home full of the news he had heard in New York.

"Just as I thought," he said to himself, "Chester Rand ought never to have left Wyncombe. He ain't calc'lated to succeed in the city. He'd orter have stayed in my store. In two or three years he might have been earnin' four or five dollars a week, and he could have boarded at home. It costs a sight to live in the city. I ain't sure that I could afford it myself."

Mr. Tripp decided to offer Chester his old place at two dollars and a half a week. Abel Wood was again in his employ, but he didn't like him as well as Chester.

The latter he had always found reliable, while Abel was rather apt to forget what Silas told him. Once he had stopped in the street and played ball, losing ten or fifteen minutes in that way. Mr. Tripp was obliged to confess that he never had a more satisfactory boy than Chester.

The store closed at nine, and Silas, instead of going into the house, walked over to Mrs. Rand's cottage.

She was rather surprised when she saw who her visitor was.

"Good-evening, Mr. Tripp," she said, politely. "Won't you come in?"

"Thank you, widder. It's rather late to call, but I thought you might like to hear about York, seein' Chester is there."

"Have you been to New York to-day?"

"Yes; I went up on a little business."

"Did you see Chester?"

"No, I didn't see him," answered Silas, significantly.

"Did you hear anything of him?" Mrs. Rand naturally asked.

Mr. Tripp coughed.

"Well, yes, I heered somethin' about him."

"Is he—sick?" asked the mother, anxiously, made apprehensive by his tone.

"Not that I know of. Hain't he writ anything special to you?"

"I had a letter yesterday, but there was nothing special in it."

"I suppose he didn't say nothin' about his place?"

"Yes; he likes it very much."

"I don't like to say it, widder, but he's deceivin' you. I saw his employer myself, and he said that he had to discharge Chester."

Horatio Alger, Jr

Somehow Mrs. Rand did not seem so much disturbed by this intelligence as the storekeeper thought she would be.

"Oh, you mean the real estate office," she said.

"Yes; I was treated quite handsome by Mr. Mullins, the bookkeeper, who is runnin' the business while Mr. Fairchild is away. He says Chester wasn't spry enough, that he wasn't wide awake enough to work in the city."

Mrs. Rand actually smiled.

"So that is what he said," she returned. "I can tell you why Chester was discharged. Mr. Mullins wanted to give the place to his nephew."

"Mebbe so," answered Silas, dubiously. "Anyhow, it's unfortunate for Chester to lose his place. I feel for you, Mrs. Rand, as I always liked Chester myself, and I came here to-night to say that I'm ready to take him back into the store, and give him two dollars and a half a week. He suits me."

Mr. Tripp leaned back in the rocking-chair and looked as if he had made a very handsome proposal.

"I see, Mr. Tripp," said Mrs. Rand, smiling, "that you think Chester is out of a position."

"So he is. Wasn't he discharged? I know from what Mr. Mullins said he won't take him back."

"Chester would not be willing to go back. He has a new and better place."

"You don't say!" ejaculated Mr. Tripp, surprised and, it must be confessed, disappointed. "What sort of a place is it?"

"He is working for a New York paper or magazine."

"Sho! Does he get as much pay as he did at the other place?"

"Considerably more," Mrs. Rand answered, with satisfaction.

"More'n five dollars a week?"

"Yes; he offers to send me five dollars a week, but I can get along without assistance, since Miss Dolby pays me so liberally."

"Well, I am surprised. Chester is very lucky. Mebbe it won't last," he continued, hopefully.

"It seems likely to be permanent."

"Well, I guess I must be goin'. If he should lose his place, tell him I will take him back any time."

"I don't think he would be satisfied to come back to Wyncombe after working in New York."

Silas Tripp returned to his house rather disappointed. He had felt so sure of securing Chester's services, and now his old boy seemed to be quite out of his reach.

"Offered to send his mother five dollars a week!" he soliloquized. "Then he must be makin' as much as ten in his new place. Mr. Mullins didn't seem to know about it. I wonder what he can be doin' to get such a high salary."

CHAPTER XXVIII

PROF. NUGENT

Chester still went three times a week to the house of Prof. Hazlitt. He was getting on fast with the professor's work.

"I think I shall go to press with my book before the end of the ycar," said the professor, one evening, as Chester was taking his leave. "In my preface I shall mention your name, Chester, as my artistic collaborator."

"Couldn't you mention my name, too, Uncle Edgar?" asked Arthur Burks.

"In what way?" inquired the professor smiling.

"You can say that I supervised the illustrations," answered Arthur, demurely.

"I am afraid you will have to wait till you are better entitled to credit."

"Now, that's mean, Uncle Edgar. I know how I'll get even with you."

"How?"

"I will write a rival book, and get Chester to illustrate it better than yours."

"It would need better illustrations, since there would be nothing else in the work worthy of attention."

"Your uncle has got you there," said Chester.

"You'll illustrate my book, won't you?"

"Certainly; that is, if I can depend on prompt payment."

Chester and Arthur Burks were fast friends. Arthur did not shine in scholarship, but he was fond of fun, and was a warm-hearted and pleasant companion, and a true friend.

One afternoon he called on Chester at his room.

"I bring you an invitation to dinner," he said. "Uncle has a friend from Oregon visiting him, and as he is an interesting talker, you will enjoy meeting him. I believe he is a professor in Williamette University."

"Thank you, Arthur; I shall be very glad to come."

"Come with me now, if you have got through your day's work. You can have a little scientific conversation before dinner."

"It will be the science of baseball and tennis, I suspect, Arthur."

"No doubt you will find me very instructive."

"You always are, Arthur."

"Thank you. I like to be appreciated by somebody."

At the dinner table Chester was introduced to Prof. Nugent.

"This is Chester Rand, the young artist who is illustrating my ethnological work, brother Nugent," said Prof. Hazlitt.

"What—this boy?" Prof. Nugent exclaimed, in a tone of surprise.

"Yes. Boy as he is, he is a salaried contributor to *The Phoenix*."

"You surprise me. How old are you, Mr. Rand?"

"Sixteen."

"I suppose you began your art education early?"

Chester smiled.

"No, sir," he answered. "Four months ago I was the boy in a country grocery store."

"This is wonderful. I shall subscribe to *The Phoenix* before I go back to my Western home."

"I am afraid, sir, it will be too light to suit your taste."

"My dear young friend, don't suppose I am always grave. What says the Latin poet:

"*'Dulce est desipere in loco.'*"

"If you don't understand it, probably Arthur can enlighten you."

"What does it mean, Arthur?"

"It means, 'When all your serious work is done, 'tis best to have a little fun,'" answered Arthur, promptly.

"Bravo, Arthur," said Prof. Nugent, clapping his hands. "So we have a young poet as well as a young artist here."

"Oh, yes," answered Arthur. "I'm pretty smart, but few people find it out."

"You'd better ask the professor about Tacoma," suggested Arthur, during a pause in the conversation.

CHAPTER XXIX

MR. FAIRCHILD'S TELEGRAM

"Tacoma!" repeated the professor. "Who is interested in Tacoma?"

"I own five lots of land there," answered Chester.

"Then I congratulate you. Lots are rising there, and are destined to go to a still higher point."

"How do you account for that?" asked Prof. Hazlitt.

"In three months the Northern Pacific Railroad will be completed, and that will give a great impetus to the growth of the town. I expect to live to see fifty thousand people there. Let me ask how you became possessed of these lots?"

"They were given to me by a friend now dead."

"What was his name?"

"Walter Bruce."

"Indeed! Why, I own three lots adjoining the Bruce lots. They are among the best located in the town."

"Would you advise me to keep them or sell if I have the chance?"

"To keep them, by all means. I shall keep mine. If, however, you wish to sell, I will myself pay you five hundred dollars each."

"Then I may consider myself worth twenty-five hundred dollars," said Chester, in a tone of satisfaction.

"Yes, and more if you are willing to wait."

"I think Mr. Bruce only gave twenty-five dollars apiece for them."

"Very likely. Mine only cost thirty dollars each."

"I shall begin to look upon you as a rich man, Chester," said Arthur Burks.

"Only a rich boy," corrected Chester, laughing. "I haven't begun to shave yet."

"I think I shall commence next week," remarked Arthur, rubbing his cheek vigorously.

"Since you own property in our neighborhood, Mr. Rand," said Prof. Nugent, "why don't you make us a visit?"

"I hope to some day when I can afford it," replied Chester, "but I didn't know till you told me just now that my lots were worth more than a trifle."

"If ever you do come, don't forget to call on me at the university. It is located in Salem, Oregon. I may be able to take a trip to Tacoma with you."

"Thank you, sir. I should like nothing better."

The next afternoon Chester chanced to enter the Fifth Avenue Hotel. He went through the corridor and into the reading room to buy a paper. What was his surprise to see his recent acquaintance, Paul Perkins, sitting in an armchair, reading a Minneapolis journal.

"Why, Chester!" exclaimed Mr. Perkins, cordially, as he rose and shook Chester's hand vigorously. "It does my heart good to see you. I was intending to call at your office to-morrow."

"You wouldn't have found me, Mr. Perkins."

"How is that?"

"I have been discharged."

"By that rascal, Mullins? It's a shame. I must see if I can't find you another position."

"Thank you, but it is not necessary. I have a place already."

"Good! Is it in the real estate business?"

"No, I am engaged on *The Phoenix*, a new weekly humorous paper, as one of the regular staff of artists."

"Whew! That is good. Do you get fair pay?"

"Twenty-five dollars a week."

"You don't say so. That is surprising. How much did you get at the other place?"

"Five."

"Then this is five times as good. You ought to give Mr. Mullins a vote of thanks for bouncing you."

"I don't think he meant to benefit me," said Chester, smiling.

"Do you have to work hard? What are your hours?"

"I have none. I work at home and select my own hours."

"Are you through work for the day?"

"Yes."

"Then you must stay and dine with me. It is four o'clock. We can chat for an hour, and then go to dinner."

"Thank you. I will accept with pleasure. Did you have a pleasant journey?"

"Yes; but I should have enjoyed it better if you had been with me. I called at the White House and shook hands with the President."

"Did you tell him you wanted an office?"

"No office for me. I would rather have my own business and be my own master. Washington's a fine city, but give me Minneapolis."

"I may call on you in Minneapolis sometime, Mr. Perkins."

"I hope you will. You'll find it worth visiting. It's a right smart place, if I do say it."

"I have seen a professor from a university in Oregon, and he has given me good news of my lots in Tacoma. I have five, as I think I told you. He offered me five hundred dollars apiece cash down."

"Don't you take it! They're going a good deal higher, now that the railroad is nearly completed."

"So he told me."

"I congratulate you on your good luck, Chester. I am sure you deserve it. But you haven't told me why you were 'bounced.'"

"Mr. Mullins said I wasted time in going his errands. It wasn't true, but it was only an excuse to get rid of me. He took his cousin Felix in my place."

The two friends went to dinner about six o'clock. At seven they came downstairs and sat in the lobby on a sofa near the door.

Through the portal there was a constant ingress and egress of men—a motley crowd—business men, politicians, professionals and men perhaps of shady character, for a great hotel cannot discriminate, and hundreds pass in and out who are not guests and have no connection with the house.

"It is a wonderful place, Chester," said Mr. Perkins. "Everybody seems at home here. I suppose everybody—everybody, at least, who is presentable—in New York comes here sometime during the year."

Just then Chester uttered a little exclamation of surprise. As if to emphasize Mr. Perkins' remark, two persons came in who were very well known to the young artist. They were David Mullins and Dick Ralston.

Mullins heard the slight exclamation and turned his head in the direction of the sofa on which Chester and his friend were sitting. So did Ralston.

"Why, it's your old boy!" he said.

Mullins smiled a little maliciously. He had not heard that Chester had a place.

"I suppose you are boarding here," he said, with a little sarcasm.

"No, Mr. Mullins, but I have just dined here—with my friend, Mr. Perkins."

Mullins inclined his head slightly.

"Has he adopted you?" he asked, in a tone bordering on impertinence.

"No, sir," answered Mr. Perkins; "but if Chester ever wants me to, I will. At present he is prosperous, and requires no help or adoption."

"Oh! Have you got a place?" asked Mullins, turning to Chester.

"Yes."

"In the same business?"

"No; I am in the office of a weekly paper."

"Oh!" said the bookkeeper, disdainfully. "They pay beggarly salaries at such places."

"Then I am favored. I receive more than twice as much as I did in your office."

Chester did not care to just state how much he received.

"That can't be possible!"

"It is a fact, however. Has Mr. Fairchild returned?"

"No. Why do you want to know?"

"I have no wish to go back, Mr. Mullins. Don't be apprehensive of that. I don't wish to disturb Felix."

Dick Ralston listened with some interest to the conversation.

"It strikes me the kid has come to no harm from being discharged," he said.

"I believe this is Mr. Perkins, of Minneapolis?"

"Yes, sir," answered the Westerner, eying the gambler with a penetrating glance.

"I shall be glad to be your guide if you wish to see something of New York. Will you join us this evening?"

"You are very polite, but I have an engagement with Chester."

"A mere boy! He knows nothing about the city."

"Still I am satisfied with him."

The two passed on and went into the bar-room, where they sat down at a table and ordered some liquid refreshment.

"Well, Mullins," said the gambler, "I am getting impatient. The days are slipping by, and you have done nothing."

"You know what I am waiting for. Yesterday a check for a thousand dollars was paid in at the office, and deposited in the bank to-day."

"Good! And then?"

"I will send Felix to the bank and draw out sixteen hundred. Will that satisfy you?"

"I see, and, according to our arrangement, Felix will hand it to me on his way back to the office, and then swear that it was taken from him by some unknown party. You have coached him, have you?"

"Yes. Of course, I had to let him into the secret partially, promising him twenty-five dollars for himself."

"Ten would have been sufficient."

"He would not have been satisfied. We can spare that."

"How soon do you expect Fairchild back?"

"In three days."

But on the morrow Mullins was disconcerted by receiving the following telegram:

"Expect me back sometime to-day. FAIRCHILD."

CHAPTER XXX

THE ATTEMPTED ROBBERY

Dick Ralston was in the real estate office when the telegram was received. Indeed, he spent a good deal of his time there, so that it was supposed by some that he had a share in the business.

"Look at that, Dick!" said the bookkeeper, passing the telegram to his confederate.

"Confusion! What sends him home so soon?" said Ralston. "Do you suppose he suspects anything?"

"No. How can he? Perhaps," said Mullins, nervously, "we had better give up the whole thing. You see how I will be placed. I'm afraid I shall be suspected."

"Look here!" growled Ralston, "I don't want to hear any such weak, puerile talk. How do you propose to pay me the nine hundred and sixty-odd dollars you owe me? Do you expect to save it out of your salary?" he concluded, with a sneer.

"I wish we had never met," said the bookkeeper, in a troubled tone.

"Thank you; but it is too late for that. There is nothing to do but to carry out our program. How much money is there on deposit in the bank?"

"About twenty-four hundred dollars."

"Then we had better draw out more than eighteen hundred. As well be hanged for a sheep as for a lamb."

"You forget, Ralston, that such a wholesale draft will raise suspicion at the bank."

"You're awfully cautious."

"I don't want everything to miscarry through imprudence."

"Come, it is ten o'clock. Better send Felix to the bank."

"Better wait a little while. If we drew such a large amount just at the beginning of banking hours, the bank officers might suspect something."

"Cautious again. Well, wait half an hour, if you must. Call Felix and give him his instructions."

Felix Gordon came in at this moment, and was admitted to the conference.

"Felix," said the bookkeeper, "you remember the arrangement I made with you yesterday?"

"Yes, Cousin David."

"It is to be carried out to-day. I shall give you a check for eighteen hundred dollars, and you will receive the money and come from the bank here."

"Yes, Cousin David."

"You will carry the parcel in the left-hand pocket of your sack coat, and if it is taken you can appear to be unconscious of it."

"Yes."

"And—that is all you will have to do, except to say that a tall, thin man"—Ralston was short and sturdy—"jostled against you, and must have taken it."

"All right! I see. And I am to have twenty-five dollars for—"

"Your trouble. Yes."

"Give it to me now."

"Wait till you come back. Don't be afraid. You will get it."

"All right."

When Felix was on his way to the bank, he did not know that he was followed at a little distance by a small man with keen, black eyes, who, without appearing to do so, watched carefully every movement of the young office boy.

When Felix entered the bank, he also entered the bank, and stood behind Felix in the line at the paying teller's window.

He nodded secretly to the teller when that official read the check presented by Felix.

"Eighteen hundred dollars?" the latter repeated, aloud.

"Yes, sir," answered Felix, composedly.

"I shall have to go back to get it. We haven't as much here."

He went to another part of the bank and returned after a time with three packages. One was labeled one thousand dollars, another five hundred dollars and a third two hundred dollars. Then he counted out from the drawer beside him a hundred dollars in bills.

Felix, with a look of relief, took the three parcels and dropped them carelessly in the side pocket of his sack coat, and put the bills in loose. Then he started on his way back to the office.

Mr. Sharpleigh, for it was he, as the reader has doubtless guessed, walked closely behind him. He was not quite sure as to the manner in which the money was to be taken, but guessed at once when he caught sight of Dick Ralston at a little distance with his eyes intently fixed upon Felix.

The office boy sauntered along, with nothing apparently on his mind, and finally stopped in front of a window on Union Square, which appeared to have considerable attraction for him.

Then it was that the detective saw Ralston come up, and, while apparently watching the window also, thrust his hand into the pocket of the office boy and withdraw the package of money, which he at once slipped into his own pocket.

Mr. Sharpleigh smiled a little to himself.

"Very neat!" he soliloquized, "but it won't go down, my cunning friend."

Felix gave a little side glance, seeing what was going on, but immediately stared again in at the window.

Sharpleigh beckoned to a tall man, dressed as a civilian, but really an officer in plain clothes.

"Go after him!" he said, in a low voice, indicating Ralston.

Then he followed Felix, who in about five minutes began to show signs of agitation.

He thrust his hand wildly into his pocket, and looked panic-stricken.

"What is the matter, my boy?" asked Sharpleigh, blandly.

"Oh, sir, I have been robbed," faltered Felix.

"Robbed—of what?"

"I had eighteen hundred dollars in bank bills in my pocket, in four parcels, and—and they must have been taken while I was looking in at this window."

"You seem to have been very careless?" said Sharpleigh. "Why were you not more careful when you knew you had so much money in your care?"

"I—I ought to have been, I know it, sir, but I wasn't thinking."

"Where are you employed?"

"At Mr. Fairchild's office, on Fourteenth Street."

"The real estate agent?"

"Yes, sir."

"I know the place."

"My cousin is the bookkeeper. He will be so angry with me."

"I think he will have reason. I saw a man following you rather closely, I presume he took the money."

"Oh, won't you come back to the office with me and tell my cousin that? I am afraid he will discharge me."

"Yes, I will go with you."

So it happened that Felix and Mr. Sharpleigh went together into the office where Mullins was eagerly waiting for the return of his emissary.

"What's the matter, Felix?" he said, as the boy entered. "Have you brought the money?"

"Oh, Cousin David, I am so sorry."

"So sorry? For what?"

"I—I have lost the money. A pickpocket took it while I was looking in at a window. This gentleman was near and he saw a suspicious-looking man next to me."

"This is a strange story, Felix. We must notify the police at once. Did you see anyone likely to commit the theft, sir?"

This was, of course, addressed to Mr. Sharpleigh.

"Yes."

"You will be willing to testify to this at the police office? You see, this boy is my cousin. Mr. Fairchild is away, and I shall be blamed for this terrible loss. Why, there were eighteen hundred dollars in the parcel!"

"There were three parcels, and a roll of bills, Cousin David."

Mr. Mullins looked surprised.

"Then it was not all put in one parcel?" he said.

"No."

"That is strange. I—I don't know what to do. Mr. Fairchild has telegraphed that he will be at home sometime during the day. Probably I had better wait till he comes before notifying the police."

This he said in a questioning sort of way, as if asking Sharpleigh's advice.

"That will give the thief a chance to escape," suggested the detective.

"True. Perhaps you will be kind enough to leave word at the nearest police office. I only wish Mr. Fairchild were here."

"All right, sir," said the detective, "I will comply with your request."

He left the office, but it is needless to say that he didn't go far away.

"This is a very interesting comedy," he murmured, rubbing his hands, "a very interesting comedy, and apparently played for my benefit."

"Now, Felix," said the bookkeeper, "tell me how it all came

out. Did the paying teller look suspicious when you presented the check?"

"No. He said he hadn't as much money in the drawer, and went to the safe in the back part of the bank. He returned with three parcels of bills in brown paper, and a hundred dollars loose."

"And then you put it in your pocket?"

"Yes, Cousin David; I did exactly as you told me. I put them in my pocket and walked back in a leisurely way."

"Did you see anything of Ralston?"

"Yes, I saw him out of the corner of my eye, while I was looking in at a window on Union Square."

"He took the money?"

"Yes. Now, Cousin David, give me the twenty-five dollars."

At that instant the door was opened suddenly, and Dick Ralston dashed into the office, looking very much excited.

"Mullins," he said, "we've been sold—sold—regularly sold. Look at this!" and he showed one of the brown packages partly torn open.

"Well," said the bookkeeper, "what's the matter?"

"Matter? Matter enough. Here's a package marked one thousand dollars, and it contains only slips of green paper in place of bills. You can see for yourself."

CHAPTER XXXI

A DAY OF SURPRISES

The bookkeeper looked amazed.

He turned to Felix.

"Was this package given you at the bank?" he asked.

"Yes," answered Felix.

"I don't understand it. Do you think they suspected anything?" he continued, turning to Ralston.

"What could they suspect?" growled Dick. "It's a pretty trick for a respectable bank to play on a customer."

"Was all the money bogus?" asked Mullins.

"Here are a hundred dollars in good bills."

"Have you opened any of the other packages?"

"No, but I will."

The gambler tore off a little of the outer paper from the

five-hundred-dollar and two-hundred-dollar packages, only to discover that their contents were no more valuable than those of the first bundle.

"I'd like to know what all this means," said Ralston. "Is it a trick of yours?" he demanded, looking suspiciously at Mullins.

"No. On my honor, no. It is very puzzling. They must have made a mistake at the bank."

"Send the boy back."

"It won't do. He has already reported that he has been robbed. It's—it's very awkward."

"You must do something," said Dick Ralston, harshly. "I'm not going to be swindled in this way."

It was at this point that the office door was heard to open. Mr. Sharpleigh entered and fixed his glance on Ralston.

"Mr. Mullins," he said, "you wish to know who robbed your office boy of the money he drew from the bank?"

"Yes," faltered Mullins.

"There he stands!" answered Sharpleigh, calmly, pointing to Ralston.

"It's a—lie!" exclaimed the gambler, but he turned pale.

"I saw the robbery with my own eyes." went on the detective, "and—" he turned his eyes to the door, which opened to admit a stalwart policeman.

"Arrest that man!" said the detective. "He lay in wait for the office boy, and on his return from the bank robbed him of a large sum of money which he had just drawn out."

"Who are you?" demanded Ralston, trying to brazen it out.

"I am James Sharpleigh, a detective."

Mullins listened in dismay, for Sharpleigh's name was familiar to him as one of the cleverest detectives in the city.

"And who authorized you to meddle in a matter that did not concern you?"

The answer came from an unexpected quarter. Mr. Fairchild, valise in hand and dusty with travel, entered the office. He heard the question, and quickly comprehended the situation.

"It is nearly two weeks," he said, "since I engaged Mr. Sharpleigh to watch what was going on in the office. Chester Rand telegraphed me that he had been discharged, and my suspicions were excited."

"So it's that boy!" muttered the bookkeeper, spitefully.

"I left all to the discretion of my friend Sharpleigh, who has justified my confidence. I shall have to ask him to throw light on the present situation."

This the detective did in a few brief sentences.

"Am I to arrest this man?" asked the policeman.

"Yes," answered the broker, sternly. "Mr. Sharpleigh, will you accompany the officer and prefer charges?"

"See here," said Ralston, with an ugly look, "I'm not going to be a scapegoat. Your bookkeeper put up this job."

Mr. Fairchild turned slowly and regarded David Mullins attentively.

"I will bear in mind what you say," he answered.

"I took nothing of value," continued Ralston, "and you can't hold me. Here are three packages filled with green paper."

"Yes," said Sharpleigh, "the bank teller was acting under my instructions. I took care, however, to have one roll of genuine bills."

When the three had left the office Mr. Fairchild turned to the bookkeeper.

"Mr. Mullins," he said, "what could induce you to engage in such a wicked plot?"

"I don't admit any complicity in the affair," replied the bookkeeper, in a surly tone.

"Have you seen Chester Rand lately?"

"I saw him last evening at the Fifth Avenue Hotel."

"Why did you discharge him?"

"I thought him unfit for his place."

"There may be a difference of opinion on that point. This boy," he added, significantly, "is a relative of yours, I believe."

"Yes."

"Will you give me an idea of what has been done during my absence?"

Together the broker and the bookkeeper went over the books. Then Mr. Fairchild went out to dinner.

He was no sooner out of the office than Mullins said: "Felix, remain here till Mr. Fairchild returns. I am going out on an errand."

He opened the safe, drew therefrom a small package and left the office.

Half an hour later he was on a Cortlandt Street ferryboat bound for the Jersey shore.

The package which he took with him contained four hundred dollars in bills, which he had drawn from the bank the day previous without the knowledge of his confederate. He had been providing for contingencies.

When Mr. Fairchild returned Felix delivered the message.

The broker at once looked suspicious.

"Did Mr. Mullins say where he was going?" he asked.

"Yes, sir. He said he was going out on an errand."

"Did he take anything with him?"

"I didn't observe, sir."

When Sharpleigh came in a little later he looked about

him inquiringly.

"Where's Mullins?"

"I don't think we shall see him again very soon," and the broker told the detective what he knew about his disappearance.

Sharpleigh shrugged his shoulders.

"He has been too sharp for us," he said. "Do you want me to do anything?"

"No; his loss of place and reputation will be a sufficient punishment."

At the close of the day Felix said: "I suppose you don't want me any more."

"You can stay till the end of the week. I have not had time to form any plans."

"Do—do you think Cousin David will come back?"

"I think it very improbable," said the broker, seriously. "Can you throw any light on the events of to-day?"

"Yes, sir."

"Go on. Was the robbery planned?"

"Yes, sir. I was to receive twenty-five dollars for my share."

"I believe you know Chester Rand?"

"Yes, sir."

"Do you know where he lives?"

"Yes, sir."

"Will you ask him to call here to-morrow?"

"I will, sir; but he tells me he has a good place, and would not care to return."

"I am aware of that. It is possible I may retain you—"

"Oh, sir, if you would!"

"On condition that you agree to serve me faithfully."

This was quite beyond the expectations of Felix.

"I will try to do so," he said, earnestly.

"You have begun well by confessing your share in the plot which came so near being successful. As your day's work is ended, I will consider the errand on which I am sending you extra, and will pay you for it."

The broker handed a half dollar to Felix, which he accepted joyfully.

"I don't much care if Cousin David has gone away," he soliloquized. "Mr. Fairchild seems a good sort of man, and I'll do my best to please him."

When Felix was ushered into Chester's presence the latter was just finishing a comic sketch for *The Phoenix*.

"What's that?" asked Felix, in surprise, for he was quite unaware of Chester's artistic gifts.

Chester showed it to him with a smile.

"Now you see how I am making my living," he said.

"Do you get pay for that?"

"Yes, certainly."

Then Felix bethought himself of his errand.

"There's a great row at the office," he said. "Mr. Fairchild has got home, Cousin David has run away and Mr. Ralston is arrested."

"That's a budget of news. When did Mr. Fairchild return?"

"This forenoon. He wants you to call to-morrow."

"All right. I will do so."

"And if he offers you back your old place you won't take it?" said Felix, anxiously. "If you don't, I think he'll keep me."

"Then I'll promise not to accept. I am better satisfied where I am. Have you had supper, Felix?"

"No."

"Then come and take supper with me. I go out about this time."

"It had certainly been a day of surprises," as Felix reflected when he found himself seated opposite a boy whom he had always disliked, as his guest.

CHAPTER XXXII

EDWARD GRANGER

"I suppose you don't care to come back to the office, Chester?" said Mr. Fairchild, when Chester called upon him the next day at the office.

"I like my present position better," answered Chester; "besides, I suppose you are hardly prepared to offer me twenty-five dollars a week."

"Do you receive as much as that?" asked the broker, in amazement.

"Yes, sir."

"I congratulate you heartily," said Mr. Fairchild. "It is clear that you are too high priced for the real estate business."

"Felix tells me you may retain him."

"I will give him a chance. It depends upon himself whether he stays."

"I am very glad of it, sir. Felix has hardly been my friend, but now that his cousin is away he may improve. I certainly hope so."

"What shall you do about Ralston?" asked Chester, presently.

"I shall proceed against him. Such a man is a curse to the community. It was through him that my bookkeeper lost his integrity and ruined his prospects. If he is locked up he will be prevented from doing any more harm."

As Dick Ralston will not again figure in this story, it may be mentioned here that he was found guilty in the trial that soon followed, and was sentenced to a term of several years' imprisonment.

The bitterest reflection he had when sentence was pronounced was that his confederate, Mullins, had escaped and was a free man. Rogues may work together, but it is seldom that any tie of friendship exists between them.

Chester was now able to save money. Including what he received from Prof. Hazlitt, his income was about thirty-five dollars a week.

His personal expenses were greater than they had been, on account of having a more expensive room. Yet altogether they did not exceed twelve dollars per week, leaving him a balance of twenty-three.

Of this sum he proposed to send his mother a part, but she wrote that the liberal board paid by Miss Jane Dolby covered all her expenses.

"I hope if you have money to spare you will put it in some savings bank," she wrote. "At present we are well and prospering, but the time may come when our income will be diminished, and then it will be very comfortable to have some money laid aside."

Chester acted upon his mother's suggestion. He did not tell her how much he earned. He wished this to be an agreeable surprise at some future day.

Then Chester moved into a larger room. The hall bedroom which he had hitherto occupied was taken by a young man of nineteen named Edward Granger. He was slender and looked younger than he was.

He did not seem strong, and there was a sad expression on his face. Sometimes he called on Chester, but for several days they had not met. About six o'clock one afternoon Chester knocked at his door.

"Come in!" he heard, in a low voice.

Entering, he saw Edward lying on the bed face downward, in an attitude of despondency.

"What's the matter, Edward?" he asked. "Are you sick?"

"Yes, sick at heart," was the sad reply.

"How is that?" inquired Chester, in a tone of sympathy.

"I have lost my place."

"When was that?"

"Three days since. My employer has engaged in my place a boy from the country—his nephew—and I am laid aside."

"That is unfortunate, certainly, but you must try to get another place. Your employer will give you a recommendation, won't he?"

"Yes, I have one in my pocket, but it is not easy to get a new place, and meanwhile—" He hesitated.

"Meanwhile you are out of money, I suppose," said Chester.

"Yes; I couldn't save anything. I got only five dollars a week, and my room costs two. I suppose, when the week is up, Mrs. Randolph will turn me into the street."

"Not while you have a friend in the next room," said Chester, cordially.

Edward looked up quickly.

"Will you really be my friend?" he asked.

"Try me. Have you had supper?"

"I have not eaten anything for two days," answered Granger, sadly.

"Why didn't you call upon me? I wouldn't have seen you suffer."

"I didn't like to ask. I thought you would consider me a beggar."

"You will understand me better after a while. Now put on your hat and come out with me."

Edward did so, but he was so weak from long fasting that he was obliged to lean upon Chester in walking to the restaurant, which was luckily near by.

Horatio Alger, Jr

"Let me advise you to take some soup first," said Chester. "Your stomach is weak, and that will prepare it for heartier food."

"I don't feel hungry," returned Edward. "I only feel faint."

"It may be well not to eat very much at first."

"How kind you are! I must be two or three years older than you, yet you care for and advise me."

"Consider me your uncle," said Chester, brightly. "Now tell me how it happens that you didn't apply to some friend or relative."

A shadow passed over the boy's face.

"I have none in New York—except yourself."

"Then you are not a city boy."

"No; I came from Portland."

"In Maine?"

"No; in Oregon."

"You have relatives there?"

"A mother."

"I suppose you hear from her?"

Edward Granger was silent.

"I don't wish you to tell me if you have an objection."

"Yes, I will tell you, for I think you are a true friend. My mother is married again, and my stepfather from the first disliked me. I think it is because my mother had money, and he feared she would leave it to me. So he got up a false charge against me of dishonesty. My mother became cold to me, and I—left home. I am of a sensitive nature, and I could not bear the cold looks I met with."

"How long ago was this?"

"About six months since."

"You came to New York directly?"

"Yes."

"Where did you get the money to come?"

"I came by it honestly," answered Edward, quickly. "I had a deposit in a savings bank, put in during my own father's life. I felt I had a right to use this, and I did so. It brought me to New York, and kept me here till I got a place in an insurance office."

"And you managed to live on five dollars a week?"

"Yes; it was hard, but I went to the cheapest eating houses, and I—got along."

"But you had no money to buy clothing."

"I brought a fair supply with me. Now I am beginning to need some small articles, such as handkerchiefs and socks."

"I wondered you would never go to supper with me."

"I didn't want you to know how little I ordered. You might have thought me mean."

"Poor fellow!" said Chester, pityingly. "You have certainly had a hard time. And all the while your mother was living in comfort."

"Yes, in luxury, for she is worth at least fifty thousand dollars in her own right."

"I hope your stepfather has not got possession of it."

"He had not when I came away. My mother is naturally cautious, and would not give it to him. He attributed this to my influence over her, but it was not so. She is of Scotch descent, and this made her careful about giving up her property. She allowed him the use of the income, only reserving a little for herself."

"Have you had any communication with her since you left Portland?"

"I wrote her once, but received no answer."

"The letter may not have reached her. It may have fallen into the hands of your stepfather. What is his name?"

"Trimble—Abner Trimble."

"Was he in any business?"

"Yes; he kept a liquor saloon, and patronized his own bar too much for his own good."

"I shouldn't think your mother would like to have him in that business."

"She asked him to change it, but he wouldn't. He had a set of disreputable companions who made his saloon their head-quarters, and he did not wish to give them up, as he might have had to do if he had gone into another business."

By this time supper was over, and the two walked to Broadway. Edward felt stronger, and his eye was brighter.

Suddenly he gripped Chester's arm.

"Do you see that man?" he asked, pointing to a black-bearded man on the other side of the street.

"Yes; what of him?"

"It is a gentleman from Portland, a neighbor of ours. What can he be doing in New York?"

CHAPTER XXXIII

A FRIEND FROM OREGON

"Go over and speak to him," suggested Chester.

"Come with me, then."

The two boys crossed the street and intercepted the man from Portland. He was of medium height, with dark hair, and had a brisk, Western way with him.

"Don't you remember me, Mr. Wilson?" said Edward.

"What! Edward Granger?" ejaculated the Oregonian. "Well, I am glad to see you. Didn't know what had become of you. Are you living here?"

"Yes, sir. Let me introduce my friend, Chester Rand."

"Glad to meet you, Mr. Rand," said Wilson, heartily. "So you are a friend of Edward's."

"Indeed he is, an excellent friend!" exclaimed young Granger. "Have you—seen my mother lately?"

"Come over to my hotel and I'll answer all your questions.

I'm stopping at the Continental, on the next block."

"All right! Will you come, Chester?"

"Yes; I shall be glad to."

They were soon sitting in the office of the Continental Hotel, at the corner of Broadway and Twentieth Street.

"Now I'll answer your questions," said Nathaniel Wilson. "Yes, I saw your mother the day before I set out."

"And is she well?" asked Edward, anxiously.

"She was looking somewhat careworn. She probably misses you."

"She never writes to me," said Edward, bitterly.

"It may be because she doesn't know your address. Then your stepfather keeps her prejudiced against you."

"I suppose there is no change in him?"

"No; except that he is drinking harder than ever. His business is against him, though he would drink even if he didn't keep a saloon."

"Does he treat my mother well?"

"I think he does. I have never heard anything to the contrary. You see, he wouldn't dare to do otherwise, as your mother has the property, and he wants to keep in with her in order to get a share."

"I have been afraid that she would give a part to him."

"Thus far I am confident she hasn't done it. She is Scotch, isn't she?"

"Yes; her name was Downie, and she was born in Glasgow, but came to this country at an early age."

"The Scotch are careful and conservative."

"She probably gives most of her income to Trimble—indeed, he collects her rents—but the principal she keeps in her own hands. Once I heard your stepfather complaining bitterly of this. 'My wife,' he said, 'treats me very badly. She's rolling in wealth, and I am a poor man, obliged to work early and late for a poor living.'"

"He pays nothing toward the support of the house," said Edward, indignantly. "Mother pays all bills, and gives him money for himself besides."

"I don't see how she could have married such a man!"

"Nor I. He seems coarse, and is half the time under the influence of drink."

"I wonder whether he has induced your mother to make a will in his favor," said Wilson, thoughtfully. "If he did, I think her life would be in danger."

Edward turned pale at this suggestion.

"I don't care so much for the property," he said, "but I can't bear to think of my mother's life as being in danger."

"Probably your mother's caution will serve her a good turn here also," said Wilson. "It isn't best to borrow trouble. I will keep watch, and if I see or hear of anything alarming I will write you. But now tell me about yourself. Are you at work?"

"Not just at present," replied Edward, embarrassed.

"But I think I can get him another place in a day or two," said Chester, quickly.

"If you need a little money, call on me," added the warm-hearted Westerner. "You know you used to call me your uncle Nathaniel."

"I wouldn't like to borrow," said Edward, shyly.

"When was your birthday?"

"A month ago."

"Then I must give you a birthday present You can't object to that," and Mr. Wilson took a ten-dollar gold piece from his pocket and pressed it upon Edward.

"Thank you very much. I can't decline a birthday gift."

"That's what I thought. I am an old friend, and have a right to remember you. Was Mr. Rand in the same office with you?"

"No; Chester is an artist."

"An artist! A boy like him!" ejaculated the Oregonian in surprise.

Chester smiled.

"I am getting older every day," he said.

"That's what's the matter with me," rejoined Mr. Wilson.

"You haven't any gray hair yet, while I have plenty."

"Not quite yet," smiled Chester.

"What kind of an artist are you?"

"I make drawings for an illustrated weekly. It is a comic paper."

"And perhaps you put your friends in occasionally?"

"Not friends exactly, but sometimes I sketch a face I meet in the street."

"You may use me whenever you want a representative of the wild and woolly West."

"Thank you, Mr. Wilson."

"But in that case you must send me a copy of the paper."

"I won't forget it."

"How long are you staying in New York, Mr. Wilson?" asked Edward.

"I go away to-morrow. You must spend the evening with me."

"I should like to do so. It seems good to see an old friend."

"By and by we will go to Delmonico's and have an ice cream. I suppose you have been there?"

"No; office boys don't often patronize Delmonico. They are more likely to go to Beefsteak John's."

"I never heard that name. Is it a fashionable place?"

"Yes, with those of small pocketbooks. It is a perfectly respectable place, but people living on Fifth Avenue prefer the Brunswick or Delmonico's."

Edward brightened up so much owing to the presence of a friend from his distant home that Chester could hardly believe that it was the same boy whom he had found but a short time before in the depths of despondency.

About nine o'clock they adjourned to Delmonico's and ordered ices and cake.

"This seems a tiptop place," said the Oregonian, looking about him. "We haven't got anything equal to it in Portland, but we may have sometime. The Western people are progressive. We don't want to be at the tail end of the procession. Mr. Rand, you ought to come out and see something of the West, particularly of the Pacific coast. You may not feel an interest in it at present, but—"

"I have more interest in it than you imagine, Mr. Wilson. I have some property at Tacoma."

"You don't mean it! What kind of property?"

"I own five lots there."

"Then you are in luck. Lots in Tacoma are rising every day."

"But it wouldn't be well to sell at present, would it?"

"No; the railroad has only recently been completed, and the growth of Tacoma has only just begun."

"I hope to go West some day."

"When you do you must call on me. Perhaps you will come, too, Edward?"

Edward Granger shook his head.

"It won't be worth while for me to go back while Mr. Trimble is alive. He seems to have such an influence over my mother that it would not be pleasant for me to go there and have a cold reception from her."

"I will call on her and mention your name. Then I can see how the land lays. How she can prefer such a man as Abner Trimble to her own son I can't understand."

About ten o'clock the two boys left Mr. Wilson, who had been going about all day and showed signs of fatigue.

"Shan't I see you again, Mr. Wilson?" asked Edward.

"No; I must take an early start in the morning. You had better let me lend you a little money."

"No, thank you, sir. Your generous gift will help me till I get a place."

So the farewells were said, and the boys walked home.

"Now," said Edward, "I must try to get a place. This money will last me two weeks, and in that time I ought to secure something."

He went from place to place, answering advertisements the next day, but met with no luck. He was feeling rather depressed when Chester came into his room.

"I have found a place for you," he said, brightly.

"You don't mean it! Where is it?" asked young Granger.

"At the office of *The Phoenix*. You will be in the mailing department. The salary is small—only seven dollars a week—but—"

"I shall feel rich. It is two dollars more than I received at my last place. When am I to go to work?"

"To-morrow. The mailing clerk has got a better place, and that makes an opening for you."

"And I owe this good fortune to you," said Edward, gratefully. "How can I repay you?"

"By being my friend!"

"That I shall be—for life!" replied Edward, fervently.

CHAPTER XXXIV

AFTER A YEAR

A year passed. Chester remained in the service of *The Phoenix*, which had become an established success. His artistic work was so satisfactory that his salary had been raised from twenty-five to thirty dollars per week. Yet he had not increased his personal expenses, and now had nearly a thousand dollars deposited in different savings banks.

He had concealed the extent of his prosperity from his mother, meaning in time to surprise her agreeably.

About this period he received a letter from Wyncombe. It was from his mother. It ran thus:

"DEAR CHESTER: I am sorry to write you bad news. Miss Jane Dolby has decided to visit a sister in Chicago and remain a year. Of course this cuts off the liberal income I have received from her, and which has been adequate to meet my expenses. I may be able to earn something by sewing, but it will be only a little. I shall, therefore, have to accept the offer you made me sometime since to send me a weekly sum. I am sorry to be a burden to you, but it will only be for a year. At the end of that time Miss Dolby promises to come back and resume boarding with me.

"I think we have reason to feel grateful for your continued success in New York. Silas Tripp called a few evenings since. He has had a great deal of trouble with boys. He says he has not had anyone to suit him since you left. He asked me if I thought you would come back for four dollars a week. This he seemed to consider a very liberal offer, and it was—for him. I didn't give him any encouragement, as I presume you prefer art to the grocery business.

"You need not begin to send me money, at once, as I have been able to save a little from Miss Dolby's board.

"Your affectionate mother,

"SARAH RAND."

Chester answered at once:

"DEAR MOTHER: Don't feel any anxiety about your loss of income through Miss Dolby's departure, and don't try to earn any money by sewing. My income is larger than you suppose, and I will send you weekly as much as you have been accustomed to receive from your boarder. Should it be more than you need, you can lay aside any surplus for future use.

"Tell Mr. Tripp I prefer New York to Wyncombe as a place of business, and I am obliged to decline his generous offer. I cannot help thinking sometimes how fortunate it was that he declined over a year since to increase my pay, as in that case I might still have been working for him instead of establishing a reputation as an artist here. Last week I received a larger offer from another publication, but as the publishers of *The Phoenix* have always treated me well, I didn't think that I would be justified in making a change. I mean in a week or two to come home to pass Sunday. I shall feel delighted to see my friends in Wyncombe, and most of all, my mother.

"Your loving son, CHESTER ."

Mrs. Rand protested against Chester sending her eight dollars a week, but he insisted upon it, advising her to lay aside what she did not need.

One evening about this time Edward Granger, who still occupied the small apartment adjoining, came into Chester's room, looking agitated.

"What is the matter?" asked Chester. "Have you had bad news?"

"Yes; I have had a letter from Mr. Wilson, of Portland, whom you recollect we met about a year ago."

"I remember him."

"I will read you his letter. You will see that I have reason to feel anxious."

The letter ran as follows:

"DEAR EDWARD: I promised to send you any news I might pick up about your mother and her premising husband. Trimble is indulging in liquor more than ever, and I don't see how he can stand it unless he has a castiron constitution. From what I hear he has never given up trying to get your mother's property into his hands. She has held out pretty firm, but she may yield yet. I hear that he is circulating reports that you are dead. In that case he thinks she may be induced to make a will leaving her property to Mr. Trimble; having, as I believe, no near relatives, so that he would seem to   be the natural heir.

"I may be doing Trimble an injustice, but I think if such a will were made she wouldn't live long. Your stepfather is in great straits for money, it seems, and he might be tempted to do something desperate. As far as I can hear, Abner Trimble's plan is this: He took a pal of his around to the house who had been in New York recently, and the latter gave a circumstantial account of your dying with typhoid fever. Evidently your mother believed it, for she seemed quite broken down and has aged considerably since the news. No doubt her husband will seize this opportunity to induce her to make a will in his favor. Here lies the danger; and I think I ought to warn you of it, for your presence here is needed to defeat your stepfather's wicked plans. Come out at once, if you can.

"Your friend,

"NATHANIEL WILSON."

"What do you think of that, Chester?" asked Edward, in a troubled voice.

"I think it very important. Your mother's life and your interests both are in peril."

"And the worst of it is that I am helpless," said Edward, sadly. "I ought to go out there, but you know how small my salary is. It has required the utmost economy to live, and I haven't as much as five dollars saved up. How can I make such a long and costly journey?"

"I see the difficulty, Edward, but I need time to think it over. To-morrow afternoon come in and I may have some advice to give you."

"I know that you will advise me for the best, Chester."

"There is a good deal in age and experience," said Chester, smiling.

When Edward left the room Chester took from his pocket a letter received the day previous, and postmarked Tacoma. It was to this effect:

"MR. CHESTER RAND.

"DEAR SIR: We learn that you own five lots on Main Street, numbered from 201 to 205. We have inquiries as to three of those lots as a location for a new hotel, which it is proposed to erect at an early date. We are, therefore, led to ask whether you are disposed to sell, and, if so, on what terms. We should be glad to have a personal interview with you, but if it is impracticable or inconvenient for you to come on to Tacoma we will undertake, as your agents, to carry on the negotiations.

"Yours respectfully,

"DEAN & DOWNIE,
"Real Estate Agents."

"Why shouldn't I go to Tacoma?" thought Chester. "I can probably sell the lots to better advantage than any agents, and should be entirely unable to fix upon a suitable price unless I am on the ground. In case I go on, I can take Edward with me, and trust to him to repay the money advanced at some future time."

The more Chester thought of this plan the more favorable it struck him.

He went the next day to the office of *The Phoenix*, and after delivering his sketches, said: "I should like leave of absence for two months. Can you spare me?"

"Does your health require it, Mr. Rand?" asked the editor.

"No," answered Chester, "but I own a little property in Tacoma, and there are parties out there who wish to buy. It is important that I should go out there to attend to the matter."

The editor arched his brows in astonishment.

"What!" he said. "An artist, and own real estate? This is truly surprising."

"I didn't earn it by my art," replied Chester, smiling. "It was a bequest."

"That accounts for it. I suppose, under the circumstances, we must let you go; but why need you give up your work? Probably ideas and suggestions may come to you while you are traveling. These you can send to us by mail."

"But I can't do enough to earn the salary you pay me."

"Then we will pay according to the amount you do."

"That will be satisfactory."

"Do you need an advance for the expenses of your journey?"

"No; I have some money laid by."

"Another surprise! When do you want to start?"

"As soon as possible. I will not come to the office again."

"Then good luck and a pleasant journey."

When Edward Granger came into his room later in the day, Chester said: "Day after to-morrow we start for Oregon. Ask your employers to hold your place for you, and get ready at once."

"But the money, Chester?" gasped Edward.

"I will advance it to you, and you shall repay me when you can."

CHAPTER XXXV

PREPARING FOR THE JOURNEY

No sooner had Chester decided upon his Western journey than he telegraphed to Dean & Downe, of Tacoma:

"I will call upon you within two weeks."

Mrs. Rand was much surprised when Chester, coming home unexpectedly, announced his intentions.

"Do you want me to take you with me, mother?" asked Chester, with a smile.

"I am afraid I could not help you much. But you are not used to traveling. You may take the wrong cars."

Again Chester smiled.

"I have spent over a year in the city, mother," he said. "I have got along pretty well in the last twelve months, haven't I?"

"Yes; but suppose you were to fall sick, with no one to look after you?"

"I didn't tell you that I am going to have company. Edward Granger, who was born in Oregon, and is three years older than myself, will go with me."

"Then I shall feel easier. He knows the way, and can look after you."

Chester was secretly of opinion that he was more competent to look after Edward, but did not say so. He saw that his mother was easier in mind, and this relieved him.

Before he started from New York he called to see Mr. Fairchild. On Fourteenth Street he fell in with Felix Gordon.

"How are you getting along, Felix?" he asked.

"Pretty well. Mr. Fairchild has raised me to six dollars a week."

"I am glad of it. That shows he is satisfied with you."

"I try to please him. I began to think that is the best policy. That is why you have succeeded so well."

"Do you ever hear from Mr. Mullins?"

"No; but I know where he is."

"Where? Of course you know that I have no wish to injure him."

"He is somewhere in Oregon, or perhaps in Washington Territory."

Washington had not at that time been advanced to the dignity of a State.

"That is curious."

"Why is it curious?"

"Because I am going to start for Oregon and Washington to-night."

"You don't mean it! What are you going for?"

"On business," answered Chester, not caring to make a confidant of Felix."

"Won't it cost a good deal of money?"

"Yes; but I expect to get paid for going."

"What a lucky fellow you are!" said Felix, not without a trace of envy. "I wish I could go. I like to travel, but I have never had a chance."

Mr. Fairchild was equally surprised when told of Chester's plans.

"Are you going as an artist?" he asked.

"No; as a real estate man," answered Chester. "I own a few lots in Tacoma, and have a chance of selling a part of them."

Then he went into particulars.

"I congratulate you. I have only one piece of advice to offer. Make careful inquiries as to the value of property. Then ask a fair price, not one that is exorbitant. That might drive the hotel people to seeking another site for their house."

"Thank you, Mr. Fairchild; I will remember your advice."

"The journey is an expensive one. If you need two or three hundred dollars I will loan it to you cheerfully."

"Thank you very much, but I have more money saved up than I shall require."

"I see you are careful and provident. Well, Chester, I wish you every success."

"I am sure of that, Mr. Fairchild. By the way, I hear that your old bookkeeper is in Oregon or Washington."

"Who told you?"

"Felix. Have you any message for him if I happen to meet him?"

"Say that I have no intention of prosecuting him. If he is ever able I shall be glad to have him return the money he took from me. As to punishment, I am sure he has been punished enough by his enforced flight and sense of wrongdoing."

CHAPTER XXXVI

A GREAT SURPRISE

From New York to Tacoma is a long journey. Over three thousand miles must be traversed by rail, but the trip is far from tiresome. Chester and his companion thoroughly enjoyed it. All was new and strange, and the broad spaces through which they passed were full of interest.

They stopped at Niagara Falls, but only for a few hours, and spent a day in Chicago. Then they were whirled onward to St. Paul and Minneapolis, and later on over the broad plains of North Dakota and through the mountains of Montana.

"I never thought the country was so large before," said Chester to Edward. "You have been over the ground once before."

"Yes; but part of it was during the night, It is pleasant to see it once more. Many of the places have grown considerably, though it is only two years since I came from Portland."

Chester made some agreeable acquaintances. An unsociable traveler misses many of the profitable results of his journey, besides finding time hang heavily on his hands.

　　　　　　Horatio Alger, Jr

Just after leaving Bismarck, in North Dakota, Chester's attention was called to an old man, whose white hair and wrinkled face indicated that he had passed the age of seventy years.

The conductor came through the car, collecting tickets. The old man searched for his, and an expression of dismay overspread his face.

"I can't find my ticket," he said.

"That is unfortunate. Where did you come from?"

"From Buffalo."

"When did you last see your ticket?"

"I stopped over one night in Bismarck, and had to share my room with a young man, for the hotel was crowded. I think he must have picked my pocket of the ticket."

"Did you know the ticket was missing when you boarded the train?"

"No, sir. I did not think to look."

"Your case is unfortunate. How far are you going?"

"To Tacoma. I have a son there."

"I am afraid you will have to pay the fare from here. I have no discretion in the matter, and cannot allow you to ride without a ticket."

"Don't you believe my ticket was stolen?" asked the old man, in a state of nervous agitation.

"Yes, I believe it. I don't think a man of your age would deceive me. But I cannot let you travel without paying for another."

"I haven't money enough," said the old man, piteously. "If you will wait till I reach Tacoma my son will give me money to pay you."

"I am not allowed to do that. I think you will have to get out at the next station."

The old man was much agitated.

"It is very hard," he sighed. "I—I don't know what to do."

Chester had listened to this conversation with great sympathy for the unfortunate traveler, on account of his age and apparent helplessness.

"How much is the fare to Tacoma from this point?" he asked.

"In the neighborhood of fifty dollars," answered the conductor.

"Will your son be able to pay this?" asked Chester.

"Oh, yes," answered the old man. "William has been doin' well. He is going to build a large hotel in Tacoma—he and another man."

"Then," said Chester, "I will advance you what money you need. You can give me a memorandum, so that I can collect it from your son."

"Heaven bless you, young man!" said the old man, fervently. "You are indeed a friend to me who am but a stranger. I am sure you will prosper."

"Thank you."

"What a fellow you are, Chester!" said Edward. "You will make yourself poor helping others."

"I shall sleep better for having aided the old man," answered Chester.

The rest of the journey was uneventful. The two boys went at once to Tacoma, as Chester felt that the gentlemen who were negotiating for his lots were probably in a hurry to arrange for the building of the hotel. After establishing themselves at a hotel and eating dinner, they went at once to the office of Dean & Downie, the real estate agents from whom Chester had received a letter.

Here a surprise awaited him.

Standing at a desk in the rear of the office was a figure that looked familiar. The man turned as the door opened to admit Chester, and the latter recognized to his great astonishment his old enemy—David Mullins!

CHAPTER XXXVII

DAVID MULLINS AGAIN

When David Mullins saw Chester enter the office he turned pale, and looked panic-stricken.

"You here!" he exclaimed, in a hollow voice.

"Yes, Mr. Mullins. I am surprised to meet you."

"Then you didn't know I was here?"

"I heard from Felix that you were in this part of the country."

"I am trying to earn an honest living," said Mullins, in agitation. "My employers know nothing to my prejudice. Do you come as a friend or an enemy?"

"Mr. Mullins, I haven't the least intention of harming you. I will not even appear to know you. I came here to see Dean & Downie, with whom I have business."

"Heaven be praised! I will not soon forget your kindness. Here comes Mr. Dean. Remember your promise."

At this moment Mr. Dean entered the office. David Mullins

Horatio Alger, Jr

had returned to his desk.

"This young man wishes to see you, Mr. Dean," he said, formally, when his employer entered.

Mr. Dean looked at Chester, inquiringly.

"I am Chester Rand, with whom you have had some correspondence," said Chester, tendering his card. "I have just arrived from New York."

The broker regarded him in surprise.

"You Chester Rand?" he exclaimed. "Why, you are a boy."

"I must plead guilty to that indictment," said Chester, smiling, "but I am the owner of the lots which I understand are wanted for the new hotel."

David Mullins, who heard this conversation, looked up in amazement. He had not known of the correspondence with Chester, as Mr. Dean had written his letter personally, and it had not gone through the office.

"Can you furnish any evidence of this?" asked Mr. Dean.

"Here is the letter you sent me, and here is a copy of my reply."

The broker took the letter from Chester's hand and all doubt vanished from his countenance.

"I am glad to see you here so soon, Mr. Rand," he said, "as the parties with whom I am negotiating are anxious to conclude matters as soon as possible. Will you go over with me to Mr. Taylor's office? Taylor and Pearson are the parties' names."

"I will go with pleasure."

As they walked through the chief business street Chester noticed with interest evidences of activity everywhere. Tacoma he found was situated, like San Francisco, on a side hill, sloping down toward Puget Sound.

"What a fine location for a town," he said.

"Yes," answered Mr. Dean, "this is destined to be a large city. Our people are enterprising and progressive. Seattle is at present ahead of us, but we mean to catch up, and that ere many years."

"At what price are lots selling on this street?"

"I see you have business ideas," said the broker, smiling. "I suppose you want to know what price you can charge for your lots."

"You are right."

"Of course it will not be right for me to advise you, being employed by the other party, but I will give you some idea. The lot adjoining your plot sold last week for two thousand dollars."

"Two thousand?"

"Yes."

"Probably it would be well for me to wait a year or two, as the lots would undoubtedly command more then."

"That is one way of looking at it. Let me point out another. You have five lots, have you not?"

"Yes, sir."

"If you sell three to the hotel company you can hold the other two five years if you like. The proximity of the hotel will help to enhance their value."

"I see that."

"That is a point to be considered. If you ask a prohibitory price, the hotel will go elsewhere, and you may have to wait a good while before you have a chance to sell. But here is Mr. Taylor's office."

The broker entered, followed by Chester. Here a surprise awaited him.

Sitting in an armchair was his venerable friend of the train, appearing very much at home. His face lighted up when Chester came in.

"William," he said to a stout man of middle age, "this is the young man who generously advanced money to meet my car fare when I was in danger of being put off the train."

The younger man advanced and cordially offered his hand.

"My boy," he said, "I shall not soon forget your kindness to my father. I will gladly repay you for the money you disbursed on his account."

"I was very glad to stand his friend, sir," returned Chester, modestly.

"Let me know to whom I am indebted."

"Mr. Taylor," said the broker, "this young gentleman is Chester Rand, owner of the lots which you wish to buy."

"Is it possible?" ejaculated William Taylor. "I didn't know that the owner of the lots was a boy."

"The lots were a bequest to me from the original owner," said Chester.

"And you have never been out this way before?"

"This is my first visit to Tacoma."

"You are hardly old enough to be in business."

"I am an artist; that is, I furnish illustrations to a comic weekly paper in New York."

"You have begun life early. I suspect you are better fitted for business than most young men of your age. Here is my partner, Mr. Pearson."

In the negotiation that followed the reader will not be interested. At length a mutually satisfactory arrangement was made. Chester agreed to sell the three lots wanted for the hotel for eight thousand dollars, half cash and the balance on a year's time at twelve per cent. interest.

When the business was concluded and papers signed, Mr. Dean said: "Mr. Rand, I think you have made a good bargain. You might have extorted more, but you have received a fair price and retained the good will of the purchaser. What do you propose to do with the four thousand dollars you will receive in cash?"

"I have not had time to think."

"I will venture to give you some advice. My partner, John Downie, has made a specialty of city property, and he will invest any part for you in lower-priced city lots, which are sure to advance rapidly."

"Then I will put the matter in his hands and rely on his judgment. I will carry back with me a thousand dollars, and leave with him three thousand dollars for investment."

"Then come back to the office and I will introduce you to Mr. Downie, with whom you can leave instructions."

Chester was presented to Mr. Downie, a blond young man, who looked honest and reliable, and they soon came to an understanding. They walked about the town—it was not a city then—and Chester picked out several lots which he was in favor of buying.

He remained a week in Tacoma, and before the end of that time all arrangements were perfected, and he found himself the owner of seven lots, more or less eligible, in addition to the two he had reserved in the original plot.

On the evening of the second day, as he was taking a walk alone, he encountered David Mullins.

"Good-evening, Mr. Mullins," he said, politely.

"Good-evening, Chester," returned the bookkeeper, flushing slightly. "I want to thank you for not exposing my past misdeeds."

"I hope, Mr. Mullins, you did not think me mean enough to do so."

"I am sorry to say that according to my sad experience eight out of ten would have done so, especially if they had reason, like you, to complain of personal ill treatment."

"I don't believe in persecuting a man."

"I wish all were of your way of thinking. Shall I tell you my experience?"

"If you will."

"When I left New York I went to Chicago and obtained the position of collector for a mercantile establishment. I was paid a commission, and got on very well till one unlucky day I fell in with an acquaintance from New York.

"'Where are you working?' he asked.

"I told him.

"The next day my employer summoned me to his presence.

"'I shall not require your services any longer,' he said.

"I asked no questions. I understood that my treacherous friend had given me away.

"I had a few dollars saved, and went to Minneapolis. There I was undisturbed for six months. Then the same man appeared and again deprived me of my situation."

"How contemptible!" ejaculated Chester, with a ring of scorn in his voice.

"Then I came to Tacoma, and here I have been thus far undisturbed. When I saw you I had a scare. I thought my time had come, and I must again move on."

"So far from wishing to harm you, Mr. Mullins," said Chester, "if, through the meanness of others you get into trouble you can any time send to me for a loan of fifty dollars."

"Thank you," ejaculated Mullins, gratefully, wringing Chester's hand. "You are heaping coals of fire on my head."

"You will always have my best wishes for your prosperity. If ever you are able, repay the money you took from Mr. Fairchild, and I will venture to promise that he will forgive you."

"With God's help I will!"

CHAPTER XXXVIII

ABNER TRIMBLE'S PLOT

Just off First Street, in Portland, Ore., is a saloon, over which appears the name of the proprietor:

"Abner Trimble."

Two rough-looking fellows, smoking pipes, entered the saloon. Behind the bar stood a stout, red-faced man. This was Trimble, and his appearance indicated that he patronized the liquors he dispensed to others.

"Glad to see you, Floyd," said Trimble.

"That means a glass of whisky, doesn't it?" returned Floyd.

"Well, not now. I want you to go up to the house again, to see my wife."

"About the old matter?"

"Yes; she isn't quite satisfied about the kid's death, and she won't make a will in my favor till she is. She wants to ask you a few questions."

Floyd made a wry face.

"She's as bad as a lawyer. I say, Abner, I'm afraid I'll get tripped up."

"You must stick to the old story."

"What was it?"

"Don't you remember you said that the kid hired a boat to row in the harbor along with two other boys, and the boat was upset and all three were drowned?"

"Yes, I remember. It's a smart yarn, isn't it?" grinned Floyd.

"Yes, but you mustn't let her doubt it. You remember how you came to know about the drowning?"

"No, I forget."

Abner Trimble frowned.

"Look here, Floyd. You'd better remember, or you won't get the money I promised you. You were out in a boat yourself, and saw the whole thing. You jumped into the water, and tried to save the kid, but it was no use. He went to the bottom—and that was the end of him!"

"A very pretty story," said Floyd, complacently. "Won't I get somethin' for tryin' to save the kid's life?"

"As like as not. I'll suggest it to the old lady myself."

"When do you want me to go up to the house?"

"Now. The lawyer's coming at four o'clock, and I want you

to confirm Mrs. T. in her belief in the boy's death."

"It's dry talkin', Abner," said Floyd, significantly.

"Take a glass of sarsaparilla, then."

"Sarsaparilla!" repeated Floyd, contemptuously. "That's only fit for children."

"Lemon soda, then."

"What's the matter with whisky?"

"Are you a fool? Do you think Mrs. T. will believe your story if you come to her smelling of whisky?"

"You're hard on me, Abner. Just one little glass."

"You can put that off till afterward. Here, take some lemon soda, or I'll mix you a glass of lemonade."

"Well, if I must," said Floyd, in a tone of resignation.

"You can have as much whisky as you like afterward."

"Then the sooner we get over the job the better. I'm ready now."

"Here, Tim, take my place," said Abner Trimble, calling his barkeeper; "I'm going to the house for an hour. Now come along."

Abner Trimble lived in a comfortable dwelling in the nicer portion of the city. It belonged to his wife when he married her, and he had simply taken up his residence in her house. He would have liked to have lived nearer the saloon, and had suggested this to his wife, but she was attached to her home and was unwilling to move.

Trimble ushered his visitor into the sitting room and went up to see his wife. She was sitting in an armchair in the room adjoining her chamber, looking pale and sorrowful.

"Well, Mary," said Trimble, "I've brought Floyd along to answer any questions relating to poor Edward's death."

"Yes, I shall be glad to see him," answered his wife, in a dull, spiritless tone.

"Shall I bring him up?"

"If you like."

Trimble went to the landing and called out: "You can come up, Floyd."

Floyd entered the room, holding his hat awkwardly in his hands. He was not used to society, and did not look forward with much pleasure to the interview which had been forced upon him.

"I hope I see you well, ma'am," he said, bobbing his head.

"As well as I ever expect to be," answered Mrs. Trimble, sadly. "Your name is—"

"Floyd, ma'am. Darius Floyd."

"And you knew my poor son?"

"Yes, ma'am, I knew him well. Ed and I was regular cronies."

Mrs. Trimble looked at the man before her, and was mildly surprised. Certainly Edward must have changed, or he would not keep such company. But, prejudiced against her son as she had been by her husband's misrepresentations, she feared that this was only another proof of Edward's moral decadence.

"You have been in New York recently?"

"Yes; I was there quite a while."

"And you used to see Edward?"

"'Most every day, ma'am."

"How was he employed?"

This was not a question to which Mr. Floyd had prepared an answer. He looked to Mr. Trimble as if for a suggestion, and the latter nodded impatiently, and shaped his mouth to mean "anything."

"He was tendin' a pool room, ma'am," said Floyd, with what he thought a lucky inspiration. "He was tendin' a pool room on Sixth Avenue."

"He must indeed have changed to accept such employment. I hope he didn't drink?"

"Not often, ma'am; just a glass of sarsaparilla or lemon soda. Them are my favorites."

Abner Trimble turned aside to conceal a smile. He remembered Mr. Floyd's objecting to the innocent beverages mentioned, and his decided preference for whisky.

"I am glad that he was not intemperate. You saw the accident?"

"Yes, ma'am."

"Please tell me once more what you can."

"I took a boat down at the Battery to have a row one afternoon, when, after a while, I saw another boat comin' out with three fellers into it. One of them was your son, Edward."

"Did you know Edward's companions?"

"Never saw them before in my life. They was about as old as he. Well, by and by one of them stood up in the boat. I surmise he had been drinkin'. Then, a minute afterward, I saw the boat upset, and the three was strugglin' in the water.

"I didn't take no interest in the others, but I wanted to save Edward, so I jumped into the water and made for him. That is, I thought I did. But it so happened in the confusion that I got hold of the wrong boy, and when I managed to get him on board my boat, I saw my mistake. It was too late to correct it—excuse my emotion, ma'am," and Mr. Floyd drew a red silk handkerchief from his pocket and wiped his eyes; "but when I looked out and couldn't see either of the other young fellers, and realized that they were drowned, I felt awful bad."

Mrs. Trimble put her handkerchief to her eyes and moaned. The picture drawn by Mr. Floyd was too much for her.

"I wish I could see the young man whose life you saved," she said, after a pause, "Have you his name and address?"

"No, ma'am; he didn't even thank me. I didn't get even the price of a glass of—sarsaparilla out of him."

Mr. Floyd came near saying whisky, but bethought himself in time.

"I have been much interested by your sad story, Mr. Floyd," said the sorrow-stricken mother. "You seem to have a good and sympathetic heart."

"Yes, ma'am," replied Floyd; "that is my weakness."

"Don't call it a weakness! It does you credit."

Mr. Floyd exchanged a sly glance of complacency with Abner Trimble, who was pleased that his agent got off so creditably. He had evidently produced a good impression on Mrs. Trimble.

"You see, my dear," he said, gently, "that there can be no doubt about poor Edward's death. I have thought, under the circumstances, that you would feel like making a will, and seeing that I was suitably provided for. As matters stand your property would go to distant cousins, and second cousins at that, while I would be left out in the cold.

"I know, of course, that you are younger than myself and likely to outlive me, but still, life is uncertain. I don't care much for money, but I wouldn't like to die destitute, and so I asked Mr. Coleman, the lawyer, to come round. I think I hear his ring now. Will you see him?"

"Yes, if you wish it. I care very little what becomes of the property now my boy is no more."

Mr. Trimble went downstairs, and returned with a very

respectable-looking man of middle age, whom he introduced as Mr. Coleman.

CHAPTER XXXIX

MAKING A WILL

"Mr. Coleman," said Trimble, with suavity, "this is my wife, Mrs. Trimble."

The lawyer bowed.

"I believe you wish to execute a will, Mrs. Trimble?" said he.

"Yes," answered the poor mother, in a spiritless tone.

Various questions were asked in relation to the property, and then the lawyer seated himself at a table and wrote the formal part of the will.

"I understand you wish to leave the entire property to your husband?" he said, in a tone of inquiry.

"In the event of my son's death," interpolated Mrs. Trimble.

"But, my dear, he is dead," said Abner Trimble, with a slight frown.

"I would prefer to have it expressed in this way."

"I am sure," continued Trimble, annoyed, "that Mr. Coleman will consider it unnecessary."

"I see no objections to it," said the lawyer. "Of course, the son being dead, it won't count."

"Mr. Coleman," explained Mrs. Trimble, "I have no reason to doubt my poor son's death, but I didn't see him die, and there may have been a mistake."

"How can there be?" demanded Trimble, impatiently. "Didn't my friend Floyd see him drowned?"

"He may have been mistaken. Besides, he only says he did not see him after the boat upset. He may have been picked up by some other boat."

For the first time Trimble and Floyd saw the flaw in the story, which had been invented by Trimble himself.

"Was there any boat near, Floyd?" asked Trimble, winking significantly.

"No, sir; not within a quarter of a mile."

"Edward could swim. He may have reached one by swimming."

This was news to Trimble. He had not been aware that his stepson could swim.

"Under the circumstances," said the lawyer, "I think Mrs. Trimble is right."

Trimble looked panic-stricken. Knowing that Edward Granger was still living he recognized the fact that such a will would do him no good.

"If he were alive he would let us know," he said, after a pause.

"Probably he would."

"So that we may conclude he is dead."

"It might be stipulated that if the missing son does not appear within three years from the time the will is made he may be regarded as dead?" suggested the lawyer.

"One year would be sufficient, it seems to me," put in Trimble.

"I would rather make it three," said his wife.

Abner Trimble looked disappointed, but did not dare object.

The lawyer continued to write.

"I understand, then," he observed, "that you bequeath all your estate to your husband, in the event of your son being decided to be dead."

Mrs. Trimble paused to consider.

"I think," she said, "I will leave the sum of five thousand dollars to charitable purposes as a memorial of Edward."

"I don't think much of charitable societies," growled Trimble.

"Some of them do a great deal of good," said the lawyer. "Are there any particular societies which you would wish to remember, Mrs. Trimble?"

"I leave the choice to my executor," said the lady.

"Whom have you selected for that office?"

"Will you serve?" she asked.

"Then you don't care to appoint Mr. Trimble?"

"No, I think not."

"It is customary to appoint the husband, isn't it, Mr. Coleman?" asked Abner.

"It is quite often done."

"I would prefer you," said Mrs. Trimble, decidedly.

"If it will ease your mind, I will take the office, Mrs. Trimble."

"Now," said the lawyer, after a brief interval; "I will read the draft of the will as I have written it, and you can see if it meets your views."

He had about half completed reading the document when there was heard a sharp ring at the doorbell. Then there were steps on the stairs.

A terrible surprise was in store for Mrs. Trimble.

CHAPTER XL

AN UNEXPECTED SURPRISE

The door of the sitting room was opened quickly, and two boys dashed into the room. They were Edward Granger and Chester Rand.

Abner Trimble turned pale and uttered an imprecation. All his plans, so carefully laid, were menaced with ignominious defeat.

Floyd looked up in surprise, but did not comprehend the situation. In spite of the positive testimony he had given he did not even know Edward Granger by sight.

Mrs. Trimble uttered a wild cry, but her face lighted up with supreme joy.

"Edward!" she exclaimed, and half rising, opened her arms.

Her son sprang forward and embraced his mother.

"Oh, Edward!" she murmured, "are you really alive?"

"Very much alive, mother," answered Edward, with a smile.

Horatio Alger, Jr

"And I was mourning you as dead! I thought I should never see you again."

"I have not died that I am aware of, mother. Who told you I was dead?"

"Mr. Trimble and—this gentleman," looking at Floyd. "He told me he saw you drowned in New York Bay."

Edward regarded Floyd with curiosity.

"I haven't any recollection of ever seeing the gentleman," he said. "I don't know him."

"How do you explain this, Mr. Floyd?" asked Mrs. Trimble, suspiciously.

Floyd tried to speak, but faltered and stammered. He was in a very awkward position, and he realized it. Abner Trimble came to his assistance.

"You must have been mistaken, Floyd," he said. "The young man you saw drowned must have been a stranger."

"Yes," returned Floyd, grasping the suggestion. "Of course I must have been mistaken. The young man I saw bore a wonderful resemblance to Mr. Granger."

"How long is it since you saw me drowned, Mr. Floyd?" asked Edward.

"About three weeks," answered Floyd, in an embarrassed tone.

"In New York Bay?"

"Yes. You were out in a boat with two other young fellows —that is, a young man who was the perfect image of you was. The boat upset, and all three were spilled out. I saved the life of one, but the others were, as I thought, drowned. I am sorry that I was mistaken."

"Does that mean you are sorry I was not drowned?"

"No; I am sorry to have harrowed up your mother's feelings by a story which proves to be untrue."

"I suppose Mr. Trimble brought you here," said Edward, quietly. He had in former days stood in fear of his stepfather, but now, backed up by Chester, he felt a new sense of courage and independence.

"Of course I brought him here," growled Trimble. "Fully believing in my friend Floyd's story, for I know him to be a gentleman of truth, I thought your mother ought to know it."

"I was about to make my will at Mr. Trimble's suggestion, leaving him all my property," said Mrs. Trimble, regarding her husband suspiciously.

"Of course it was better to leave it to me than to second cousins whom you don't care anything about," interposed Trimble, sourly. "Come, Floyd, our business is at an end. We will go over to the saloon."

"Shan't I get anything for my trouble?" asked Floyd, uneasily, a remark which led the lawyer to regard him sharply.

"Your valuable time will be paid for," said Trimble, sarcastically.

He led the way out, and Floyd followed.

"Mrs. Trimble," said the lawyer, rising, "allow me to congratulate you on the happy event of this day. I am particularly glad that my services are not needed."

"They will be needed, Mr. Coleman. Will you do me the favor of drawing up a will leaving my entire property, with the exception of a thousand dollars, to my son, Edward, and bring it here to-morrow morning, with two trusty witnesses, and I will sign it."

"To whom will you leave the thousand dollars?"

"To my—to Mr. Trimble," answered Mrs. Trimble, coldly. "I will not utterly ignore him."

"Very well, Mrs. Trimble. I will call at half-past ten o'clock to-morrow morning."

The lawyer bowed himself out, leaving Mrs. Trimble and the boys together.

"Mother," said Edward, "I have not yet had a chance to introduce to you my friend, Chester Rand, of New York."

"I am very glad to welcome any friend of yours, Edward."

"You have reason to do so in this case, mother. But for Chester I should not have had the money to come on from New York. He paid my traveling expenses."

"He shall be repaid, and promptly, and he will accept my heartiest thanks, also. I hope, Mr. Rand, you will make your home with us while you are in Portland."

"Thank you, Mrs. Trimble, but I have already secured lodgings at a hotel. At some future time I may accept your invitation."

Chester strongly suspected that he would not be a welcome guest to Mr. Trimble when that gentleman learned that he had been instrumental in bringing home his stepson in time to defeat his plans. But he called every day till, his business being concluded, he started on his return to New York. Edward had expected to go back with him, but to this Mrs. Trimble would not listen.

"We have been separated long enough, Edward," she said. "Henceforth your place is at my side. I feel that I have done you injustice, and I want to repair it. I made a mistake in marrying Mr. Trimble, but it is too late to correct that. I will not permit him, hereafter, to separate me from my son."

"If you wish me to remain, mother, I will," rejoined Edward. "I was not happy away from you. From this time forth I will stand by you and protect you from all that is unpleasant."

Edward spoke with a courage and manliness which he had not formerly shown. It was clear that adversity had strengthened and improved him.

CHAPTER XLI

CONCLUSION

Let us go back to Wyncombe. Mrs. Greene, living near Mrs. Rand, was a lady who made it her business to know all about her neighbors' affairs. She stepped into Silas Tripp's store to buy a pound of butter.

Mr. Tripp himself waited upon her; Mrs. Greene generally had some item of news, and for this he possessed a keen relish.

"Any news, Mrs. Greene?" he asked, as he handed her the package of butter.

"I suppose you've heard that the widder Rand has lost her boarder?"

"You don't say so!" returned Silas, with genuine interest.

"Yes, it's so. I saw her go off myself yesterday afternoon, bag and baggage."

"Was she dissatisfied, do you think?"

"Like as not. The widder says she's comin' back, but I don't believe it. Between you and me, Mr. Tripp, I wonder that she stayed so long. Now, if she had been boardin' with you it would have been different."

"So it would, Mrs. Greene; so it would. I would have been willing to take her just to oblige."

"So would I, Mr. Tripp. The widder charged her a ridiculous price—eight dollars a week."

"It was extortionate. I never charged such a price."

"Nor I. Miss Dolby's board ran the house, so that Chester didn't need to send any home, and now Chester's lost his place."

"You don't say so!" ejaculated Silas, eagerly.

"Yes. Mrs. Rand told me herself that he had left his work and gone out West in search of a place. I don't see, for my part, what the widder's goin' to do."

"I'm sorry Chester's been so unlucky. But he needn't have gone out West; I'm ready to take him back into my store."

"That's very kind of you, Mr. Tripp."

"I want to help along his mother, seein' she's a widder and in hard luck."

"Shall I tell her you will take Chester back?"

"No; I'll call round and see her about it. There may be some dickerin' about the salary. Chester's got rather high notions, but I can't afford to pay extravagant prices."

Horatio Alger, Jr

"Just so. I'm sorry for the widder Rand, but she's sot too much on that boy, and thought there wasn't no other boy in Wyncombe that was equal to him. I'm sure my Fred is just as smart as he."

It was not till the next evening that Mr. Tripp found it convenient to call on Mrs. Rand. She was rather surprised by the visit, and a little curious to learn what it meant.

"Good-evenin', widder," said Silas, coughing.

"Good-evening, Mr. Tripp. Won't you step in for a few minutes?"

"Thank you. I don't care if I do. I heard yesterday from Mrs. Greene that you'd lost your boarder."

"Yes; Miss Dolby has gone to Chicago for a year. She has a sister there."

"Do you expect her back?"

"Yes, after a year."

"I wouldn't calc'late too much upon it if I were you. Women folks is mighty onsartin when they make promises."

Mrs. Rand smiled.

"You may be right, Mr. Tripp," she said.

"I hear, too, that Chester's lost his place."

"No; he has left it for a time, but he expects to go back."

"That's onsartin, too. I'm sorry for you, widder."

"Thank you, Mr. Tripp, but there's no occasion."

"You'll be rather put to it to get along, I reckon."

"Still, I have good friends in Wyncombe," said Mrs. Rand, smiling mischievously. "Now, if I were really 'put to it,' I am sure I could rely upon your assistance."

"I'm very short of money," returned Silas, alarmed at this suggestion. "Still, I've got the will to help you. If Chester's out of work, I'm ready to take him back into the store."

"I will tell him that when I write."

"Where is he now?"

"He's gone out West."

"He's made a mistake. I knew a boy that went out West some years since, and nearly starved. He came home ragged and hungry."

"I am not afraid Chester will have that experience. He had saved up some money when at work in New York."

"It won't last long, widder. It don't take long for fifty dollars to melt away. Did he have that much?"

"I think he did, Mr. Tripp."

"He'd better have put it in a savings bank and come back to Wyncombe to work for me. How soon do you expect him back?"

"Next week."

"When he comes, send him round to see me."

A few days later, Mrs. Greene went into Silas Tripp's store again.

"Well, Mr. Tripp," she said, "Chester Rand's got home."

"You don't say! If you see him, tell him to come round and see me."

"And I can tell you some more news. You know that half-acre lot that j'ins onto the widder's land?"

"The apple orchard? Yes."

"Well, Chester's bought it."

"You don't mean it! Where on earth did he get the money? Do you know what he paid?"

"Two hundred dollars."

"He'll never be able to pay for it."

"He has paid cash down. Besides, he's got a new suit of clothes and a gold watch. I don't believe he will be willing to take a place in your store."

Silas Tripp was amazed. Nay, more, he was incredulous. But it so happened that Chester himself came into the store in five minutes, and confirmed the news.

"Where did you get the money, Chester?" asked Mr. Tripp, curiously, eying the boy with unwonted respect.

"I saved it. I received high pay in New York."

"But you've lost the place?"

"Oh, no! I go back to work next week."

"How much pay do you get?"

"Thirty dollars a week."

"Don't try to fool me!" said Silas, with asperity. "It ain't creditable to deceive a man old enough to be your grandfather."

Chester smiled.

"Do you want me to bring an affidavit from my employers?" he asked.

"But it's ridiculous, payin' a boy such wages!" objected Silas.

"It would be foolish for you to pay it, Mr. Tripp; but they think me worth it."

"What sort of work do you do?"

"I make pictures. I will show you a couple," and Chester produced a copy of *The Phoenix*.

"Why, I didn't think they paid more'n a quarter apiece for such pictures."

"It's lucky for me that they pay higher than that."

"What was you doin' out West?"

"I went partly to see the country."

"I s'pose it cost you considerable money?"

"Yes, traveling is expensive."

"You'd better have put the money in the bank."

"I don't think so."

"Boys have foolish notions. I s'pose you was sorry to hear that Miss Dolby had gone away?"

"No, I want mother to have a few months' rest."

"Your mother'll miss her board."

"No, for I shall make it up to her."

"You talk as if you was rich, Chester."

"I am not so rich as you, Mr. Tripp."

"You seem to be spending more money; some day you'll be put to it to get along."

But that has not yet come. Two years have passed, and Chester is still in the employ of *The Phoenix*, but he now receives forty dollars per week. He has sold his other two lots in Tacoma for five thousand dollars each, and still has the cheaper lots he bought as an investment. He could sell these at a handsome profit, but will hold them a while longer.

About a year ago he received intelligence from Edward Granger that his stepfather had died suddenly of heart trouble, brought on by an undue use of alcoholic mixtures. Edward concluded: "Now there is nothing to mar my mother's happiness. I live at home and manage her business, besides filling a responsible place in a broker's office. We hope you will pay us a visit before long. We have never forgotten your kindness to me in my time of need."

A month since Mr. Fairchild was surprised by receiving a remittance from Tacoma. His old bookkeeper, David Mullins, remitted to him the amount he had stolen at the time of his hurried departure from New York, with interest up to date.

"I hope, Mr. Fairchild," he concluded, "you will now forgive me for my treachery. I feel great satisfaction in paying my debt. I have been assisted by a fortunate investment in outside lots. I am glad to hear that Felix is doing well. You were kind to retain him."

Felix is really doing well, and bids fair to make a good business man. He was weak and influenced to evil by his cousin; but with good surroundings he is likely to turn out creditably.

Chester retains the friendship and good opinion of his first friend, Carl Conrad, and is a favorite visitor at the house of Prof. Hazlitt, whose great work has just appeared from the press of a subscription publisher. His nephew, Arthur Burks, is now in college, and he and Chester remain intimate friends.

Silas Tripp has ceased to expect to secure the services of Chester in his store. He had never been able to understand the secret of Chester's success, but has been heard to remark: "It does beat all how that boy gets along!"

Fortunately, prosperity has not spoiled Chester. He is still the same modest and warm-hearted boy, or perhaps I should say young man, and his friends all agree that he deserves his success.

ABOUT THE AUTHOR

Horatio Alger, Jr. (January 13, 1832–July 18, 1899) was a 19th-century American author who wrote 135 dime novels.

Many of his works have been described as rags to riches stories, illustrating how down-and-out boys might be able to achieve the American dream of wealth and success through hard work, courage, determination, and concern for others. The widely-held view involves a significant simplification, as Alger's characters do not typically achieve extreme wealth, but middle-class security, stability, and solidity of reputation—that is, their efforts are rewarded with a place in society, not domination of it. He is noted as a significant figure in the history of American cultural and social ideals.

Though often repetitive, Alger's novels remain popular. As bestsellers in their own time, Alger's books rivaled those of Mark Twain in popularity.

Alger was born in Chelsea, now Revere, Massachusetts on January 13, 1832, to a stern Unitarian minister who wanted his son to follow him into the religious world. He was tutored at home by his father until the age of ten, when he was admitted to the Gates Academy in Marlborough, Massachusetts. A year after graduating Gates, he was admitted to Harvard at age 16. For the next four years he studied under Henry Wadsworth Longfellow with the intention of one day becoming a poet. After graduating he devoted himself to teaching and writing, with uneven success. Coming to the conclusion he did not like teaching, he returned to Harvard in 1857 to pursue the ministry.

Essentially, all of Alger's novels are the same: a young boy struggles through hard work to escape poverty. However it is not the hard work itself that rescues the boy from his fate, but rather a wealthy older gentleman, who has become aware of the boy and his situation as a result of some extraordinary act of bravery or honesty which the boy has performed. The older gentleman then takes the boy in as a ward. The precipitating act might be that the boy returns a large sum of money that was lost or that he rescues someone from an overturned carriage.

Despite his remarkable literary output, Alger never became rich from his writing. He gave most of his money to homeless boys and in some instances was actually conned from his earnings by the boys he tried to help. Nevertheless, by the time he died in 1899, his books could be found in virtually every home and library in America. His books may no longer be as popular today as they once were, but the moral messages they relayed were an important factor in the development of the American dream in the 20th century. At the time of his death, Alger was living with his sister Augusta in Natick, Massachusetts. She destroyed all of his personal papers.

Other books by this author

The Young Musician
Timothy Crump's Ward
Adrift in New York
Andy Grants Pluck
Bound To Rise
Brave and Bold
Cast Upon the Breakers
Do And Dare
Driven From Home
Facing The World
Frank and Fearless
Frank's Campaign
Hector's Inheritance
Helping Himself
Herbert Carter's Legacy
Jack's Ward
Joe's Luck
Joe The Hotel Boy
Making His Way
Only An Irish Boy

Paul Prescott's Charge
Paul the Peddler
Phil the Fiddler
Ragged Dick
Risen From the Ranks
Struggling Upward
The Cash Boy
The Errand Boy
The Store Boy
The Young Explorer
Try and Trust
Walter Sherwood's Probation

Choose from Thousands of 1stWorldLibrary Classics By

A. M. Barnard	Booth Tarkington	Edward Everett Hale
Ada Leverson	Boyd Cable	Edward J. O'Biren
Adolphus William Ward	Bram Stoker	Edward S. Ellis
Aesop	C. Collodi	Edwin L. Arnold
Agatha Christie	C. E. Orr	Eleanor Atkins
Alexander Aaronsohn	C. M. Ingleby	Eleanor Hallowell Abbott
Alexander Kielland	Carolyn Wells	Eliot Gregory
Alexandre Dumas	Catherine Parr Traill	Elizabeth Gaskell
Alfred Gatty	Charles A. Eastman	Elizabeth McCracken
Alfred Ollivant	Charles Amory Beach	Elizabeth Von Arnim
Alice Duer Miller	Charles Dickens	Ellem Key
Alice Turner Curtis	Charles Dudley Warner	Emerson Hough
Alice Dunbar	Charles Farrar Browne	Emilie F. Carlen
Allen Chapman	Charles Ives	Emily Bronte
Alleyne Ireland	Charles Kingsley	Emily Dickinson
Ambrose Bierce	Charles Klein	Enid Bagnold
Amelia E. Barr	Charles Hanson Towne	Enilor Macartney Lane
Amory H. Bradford	Charles Lathrop Pack	Erasmus W. Jones
Andrew Lang	Charles Romyn Dake	Ernie Howard Pie
Andrew McFarland Davis	Charles Whibley	Ethel May Dell
Andy Adams	Charles Willing Beale	Ethel Turner
Angela Brazil	Charlotte M. Braeme	Ethel Watts Mumford
Anna Alice Chapin	Charlotte M. Yonge	Eugene Sue
Anna Sewell	Charlotte Perkins Stetson	Eugenie Foa
Annie Besant	Clair W. Hayes	Eugene Wood
Annie Hamilton Donnell	Clarence Day Jr.	Eustace Hale Ball
Annie Payson Call	Clarence E. Mulford	Evelyn Everett-green
Annie Roe Carr	Clemence Housman	Everard Cotes
Annonaymous	Confucius	F. H. Cheley
Anton Chekhov	Coningsby Dawson	F. J. Cross
Archibald Lee Fletcher	Cornelis DeWitt Wilcox	F. Marion Crawford
Arnold Bennett	Cyril Burleigh	Fannie E. Newberry
Arthur C. Benson	D. H. Lawrence	Federick Austin Ogg
Arthur Conan Doyle	Daniel Defoe	Ferdinand Ossendowski
Arthur M. Winfield	David Garnett	Fergus Hume
Arthur Ransome	Dinah Craik	Florence A. Kilpatrick
Arthur Schnitzler	Don Carlos Janes	Fremont B. Deering
Arthur Train	Donald Keyhoe	Francis Bacon
Atticus	Dorothy Kilner	Francis Darwin
B.H. Baden-Powell	Dougan Clark	Frances Hodgson Burnett
B. M. Bower	Douglas Fairbanks	Frances Parkinson Keyes
B. C. Chatterjee	E. Nesbit	Frank Gee Patchin
Baroness Emmuska Orczy	E. P. Roe	Frank Harris
Baroness Orczy	E. Phillips Oppenheim	Frank Jewett Mather
Basil King	E. S. Brooks	Frank L. Packard
Bayard Taylor	Earl Barnes	Frank V. Webster
Ben Macomber	Edgar Rice Burroughs	Frederic Stewart Isham
Bertha Muzzy Bower	Edith Van Dyne	Frederick Trevor Hill
Bjornstjerne Bjornson	Edith Wharton	Frederick Winslow Taylor

Friedrich Kerst
Friedrich Nietzsche
Fyodor Dostoyevsky
G.A. Henty
G.K. Chesterton
Gabrielle E. Jackson
Garrett P. Serviss
Gaston Leroux
George A. Warren
George Ade
Geroge Bernard Shaw
George Cary Eggleston
George Durston
George Ebers
George Eliot
George Gissing
George MacDonald
George Meredith
George Orwell
George Sylvester Viereck
George Tucker
George W. Cable
George Wharton James
Gertrude Atherton
Gordon Casserly
Grace E. King
Grace Gallatin
Grace Greenwood
Grant Allen
Guillermo A. Sherwell
Gulielma Zollinger
Gustav Flaubert
H. A. Cody
H. B. Irving
H. C. Bailey
H. G. Wells
H. H. Munro
H. Irving Hancock
H. R. Naylor
H. Rider Haggard
H. W. C. Davis
Haldeman Julius
Hall Caine
Hamilton Wright Mabie
Hans Christian Andersen
Harold Avery
Harold McGrath
Harriet Beecher Stowe
Harry Castlemon
Harry Coghill
Harry Houidini

Hayden Carruth
Helent Hunt Jackson
Helen Nicolay
Hendrik Conscience
Hendy David Thoreau
Henri Barbusse
Henrik Ibsen
Henry Adams
Henry Ford
Henry Frost
Henry James
Henry Jones Ford
Henry Seton Merriman
Henry W Longfellow
Herbert A. Giles
Herbert Carter
Herbert N. Casson
Herman Hesse
Hildegard G. Frey
Homer
Honore De Balzac
Horace B. Day
Horace Walpole
Horatio Alger Jr.
Howard Pyle
Howard R. Garis
Hugh Lofting
Hugh Walpole
Humphry Ward
Ian Maclaren
Inez Haynes Gillmore
Irving Bacheller
Isabel Cecilia Williams
Isabel Hornibrook
Israel Abrahams
Ivan Turgenev
J. G.Austin
J. Henri Fabre
J. M. Barrie
J. M. Walsh
J. Macdonald Oxley
J. R. Miller
J. S. Fletcher
J. S. Knowles
J. Storer Clouston
J. W. Duffield
Jack London
Jacob Abbott
James Allen
James Andrews
James Baldwin

James Branch Cabell
James DeMille
James Joyce
James Lane Allen
James Lane Allen
James Oliver Curwood
James Oppenheim
James Otis
James R. Driscoll
Jane Abbott
Jane Austen
Jane L. Stewart
Janet Aldridge
Jens Peter Jacobsen
Jerome K. Jerome
Jessie Graham Flower
John Buchan
John Burroughs
John Cournos
John F. Kennedy
John Gay
John Glasworthy
John Habberton
John Joy Bell
John Kendrick Bangs
John Milton
John Philip Sousa
John Taintor Foote
Jonas Lauritz Idemil Lie
Jonathan Swift
Joseph A. Altsheler
Joseph Carey
Joseph Conrad
Joseph E. Badger Jr
Joseph Hergesheimer
Joseph Jacobs
Jules Vernes
Julian Hawthrone
Julie A Lippmann
Justin Huntly McCarthy
Kakuzo Okakura
Karle Wilson Baker
Kate Chopin
Kenneth Grahame
Kenneth McGaffey
Kate Langley Bosher
Kate Langley Bosher
Katherine Cecil Thurston
Katherine Stokes
L. A. Abbot
L. T. Meade

L. Frank Baum
Latta Griswold
Laura Dent Crane
Laura Lee Hope
Laurence Housman
Lawrence Beasley
Leo Tolstoy
Leonid Andreyev
Lewis Carroll
Lewis Sperry Chafer
Lilian Bell
Lloyd Osbourne
Louis Hughes
Louis Joseph Vance
Louis Tracy
Louisa May Alcott
Lucy Fitch Perkins
Lucy Maud Montgomery
Luther Benson
Lydia Miller Middleton
Lyndon Orr
M. Corvus
M. H. Adams
Margaret E. Sangster
Margret Howth
Margaret Vandercook
Margaret W. Hungerford
Margret Penrose
Maria Edgeworth
Maria Thompson Daviess
Mariano Azuela
Marion Polk Angellotti
Mark Overton
Mark Twain
Mary Austin
Mary Catherine Crowley
Mary Cole
Mary Hastings Bradley
Mary Roberts Rinehart
Mary Rowlandson
M. Wollstonecraft Shelley
Maud Lindsay
Max Beerbohm
Myra Kelly
Nathaniel Hawthrone
Nicolo Machiavelli
O. F. Walton
Oscar Wilde
Owen Johnson
P.G. Wodehouse
Paul and Mabel Thorne

Paul G. Tomlinson
Paul Severing
Percy Brebner
Percy Keese Fitzhugh
Peter B. Kyne
Plato
Quincy Allen
R. Derby Holmes
R. L. Stevenson
R. S. Ball
Rabindranath Tagore
Rahul Alvares
Ralph Bonehill
Ralph Henry Barbour
Ralph Victor
Ralph Waldo Emmerson
Rene Descartes
Ray Cummings
Rex Beach
Rex E. Beach
Richard Harding Davis
Richard Jefferies
Richard Le Gallienne
Robert Barr
Robert Frost
Robert Gordon Anderson
Robert L. Drake
Robert Lansing
Robert Lynd
Robert Michael Ballantyne
Robert W. Chambers
Rosa Nouchette Carey
Rudyard Kipling
Saint Augustine
Samuel B. Allison
Samuel Hopkins Adams
Sarah Bernhardt
Sarah C. Hallowell
Selma Lagerlof
Sherwood Anderson
Sigmund Freud
Standish O'Grady
Stanley Weyman
Stella Benson
Stella M. Francis
Stephen Crane
Stewart Edward White
Stijn Streuvels
Swami Abhedananda
Swami Parmananda
T. S. Ackland

T. S. Arthur
The Princess Der Ling
Thomas A. Janvier
Thomas A Kempis
Thomas Anderton
Thomas Bailey Aldrich
Thomas Bulfinch
Thomas De Quincey
Thomas Dixon
Thomas H. Huxley
Thomas Hardy
Thomas More
Thornton W. Burgess
U. S. Grant
Upton Sinclair
Valentine Williams
Various Authors
Vaughan Kester
Victor Appleton
Victor G. Durham
Victoria Cross
Virginia Woolf
Wadsworth Camp
Walter Camp
Walter Scott
Washington Irving
Wilbur Lawton
Wilkie Collins
Willa Cather
Willard F. Baker
William Dean Howells
William le Queux
W. Makepeace Thackeray
William W. Walter
William Shakespeare
Winston Churchill
Yei Theodora Ozaki
Yogi Ramacharaka
Young E. Allison
Zane Grey

www.ingramcontent.com/pod-product-compliance
Lightning Source LLC
Chambersburg PA
CBHW021310250626
47155CB00002B/474